D0021970

Also by Maxine Kumin

POETRY

Connecting the Dots

Looking for Luck

Nurture

The Long Approach

Our Ground Time Here Will Be Brief

The Retrieval System

House, Bridge, Fountain, Gate

Up Country

The Nightmare Factory

The Privilege

Halfway

NOVELS

The Designated Heir

The Abduction

The Passions of Uxport

Through Dooms of Love

SHORT STORIES

Why Can't We Live Together Like Civilized Human Beings?

ESSAYS

In Deep: Country Essays

To Make a Prairie: Essays on Poets, Poetry, and Country Living

ESSAYS AND STORIES

Women, Animals, and Vegetables

Selected Poems

1960–1990

W · W · Norton & Company

New York · London

Maxine Kumin

Selected Poems

1960–1990

Printed in the United States of America
First Edition

The text of this book is composed in Monotype Bell
with the display set in Bauer Bodoni
Composition by Crane Typesetting Service, Inc.
Manufacturing by The Courier Companies, Inc.
Book design by Antonina Krass

Library of Congress Cataloging-in-Publication Data

Kumin, Maxine, date.
[Poems. Selections]
Selected poems, 1960–1990 / Maxine Kumin.
p. cm.
Includes index.
ISBN 0-393-04073-9
I. Title.
PS3521.U638A6 1997
811'.54—dc20 96-42433
CIP

W. W. Norton & Company, Inc., 500 Fifth Avenue, New York, N.Y. 10110
http://www.wwnorton.com

W. W. Norton & Company Ltd., 10 Coptic Street, London WC1A 1PU

1 2 3 4 5 6 7 8 9 0

To Carol Houck Smith

Contents

from

The Nightmare Factory

from

Up Country

from

House, Bridge, Fountain, Gate

from
The Retrieval System

from Our Ground Time Here Will Be Brief

from
The Long Approach

from
Nurture

from

Halfway

Halfway

As true as I was born into
my mother's bed in Germantown,
the gambrel house in which I grew
stood halfway up a hill, or down,
between a convent and a madhouse.

The nunnery was white and brown.
In summertime they said the mass
on a side porch, from rocking chairs.
The priest came early on the grass,
black in black rubbers up the stairs
or have I got it wrong? The mass
was from the madhouse and the priest
came with a black bag to his class
and ministered who loved him least.
They shrieked because his needles stung.
They sang for Christ upon His cross.
The plain song and the bedlam hung
on the air and blew across
into the garden where I played.

I saw the sisters' linens flap
on the clothesline while they prayed,
and heard them tell their beads and slap
their injuries. But I have got
the gardens mixed. It must have been
the mad ones who cried out to blot
the frightened sinner from his sin.
The nuns were kind. They gave me cake

and told me lives of saints who died
aflame and silent at the stake
and when I saw their Christ, I cried

where I was born, where I outgrew
my mother's bed in Germantown.
All the iron truths I knew
stood halfway up a hill, or down.

Fräulein Reads Instructive Rhymes

Adapted from "Der Struwelpeter"
by Heinrich Hoffmann

First hear the story of Kaspar the rosy-cheeked.
Once he was round and fat. He ate his dinner up.
Then, see, on Monday night, nothing will Kaspar eat.
Tuesday and Wednesday, *nein!* Kaspar throws down his cup.
Watch him shrink to a stick crying *nicht!* all that week.
Sunday he whispers *nicht* and falls down dead.
Now they must bury him. In the black earth he's meek.
And by his grave they leave Kaspar his meat and bread.
Therefore, says Fräulein, slicing the sauerbraten,
eat what I fix for you. See what can happen?

Next prances Friedrich the terrible-tempered.
He pulls the wings from flies.
He wrings the chickens' necks.
See with a long horsewhip how in this picture he
lashes the maid who cries into her handkerchief.
Wait, *aber*, all is well. Here the big dog comes in.
Angry black dog bites his knee and holds fast.
Now the Herr Doktor pours Friedrich bad medicine.
Downstairs, the napkined dog eats Friedrich's liverwurst.
Child, says Fräulein, clicking her thimble cup,
good, *ja*, be good, or the dog comes to eat you up.

Now look at Konrad the little thumb-sucker.
Ach, but his poor mama cries when she warns him
the tailor will come for his thumbs if he sucks them.
Quick he can cut them off, easy as paper.
Out goes the mother and *wupp!* goes the thumbkin in.

Then the door opens. Enter the tailor.
See in the picture the terrible tongue in
his grinning red mouth! In his hands the great shears.
Just as she told him, the tailor goes *klipp und klapp.*
Eight-fingered Konrad has learned a sad lesson.
  Therefore, says Fräulein, shaking her chignon,
  suck you must not or the tailor will chop!

Here is smart Robert the flying boy, bad one.
Hui! How the storm blows and coughs in the treetops.
Mama has told him today he must stay in,
but Robert slips out with umbrella and rain cap.
Now he is flying. The wind sucks and pulls him.
See, he is carried up, smaller and smaller.
His cap flies ahead of him, no one can help him.
  Therefore, says Fräulein, smoothing her collar,
  mind me, says Fräulein. God stands up in Heaven.
  See how He watches? He snatches the bad ones.

400-Meter Freestyle

THE GUN full swing the swimmer catapults and cracks
s
i
x
feet away onto that perfect glass he catches at
a
n
d
throws behind him scoop after scoop cunningly moving
t
h
e
water back to move him forward. Thrift is his wonderful
s
e
c
ret; he has schooled out all extravagance. No muscle
r
i
p
ples without compensation wrist cock to heel snap to
h
i
s
mobile mouth that siphons in the air that nurtures
h
i
m
at half an inch above sea level so to speak.

T
h
e
astonishing whites of the soles of his feet rise
a
n
d
salute us on the turns. He flips, converts, and is gone
a
l
l
in one. We watch him for signs. His arms are steady at
t
h
e
catch, his cadent feet tick in the stretch, they know
t
h
e
lesson well. Lungs know, too; he does not list for
a
i
r
he drives along on little sips carefully expended
b
u
t
that plum red heart pumps hard cries hurt how soon
i
t
s
near one more and makes its final surge TIME: 4:25:9

Casablanca

As years unwind now reels unwind.
Gray springs out of the hair,
cheeks refill, and eyelids lighten.
Bogie, beautifully indifferent,
seduces a cigarette and womankind.

Ingrid, in perilous rain
intensified by angle shots,
is Juno, fair and fair.
Where France falls and gates clang shut
she faithfully misses the final train.

Now Vichy is dead, and Peter Lorre
less cowardly, and Greenstreet
has gone with the parrot,
and I knew a boy with sandy hair
could do the dialogue all blurry;

cigarette dangling, cheeks sucked hollow,
hands in his jacket pockets,
could do the dialogue
for drinks at any party;
went down with his destroyer, swallowed

in the other half of that real war.
The tough guy, lately dead
of cancer, holds the girl and then they kiss
for the last time, and time goes west
and we come back to where we really are.

A Hundred Nights

Dark came first and settled in
the pin oak rubbing on my screen.
Ten lightning bugs sealed in a milk
jar on my bureau winked and sulked.
I washed into a dream of a hunchback
chasing me with an empty mail sack

until the terrible mouse with wings
notched like bread knives came skittering
down the chimney next to my bed;
rudderless, raving, flapped and shied
against the ceiling, bedclothes, table.
I screamed as soon as I was able.

Father in a union suit
came a hundred sultry nights,
came like an avenging ghost.
He waved a carpetbeater, trussed
with scrolls of hearts and cupid wings,
a racket with rococo strings.

Two uncles one floor up ran down
a hundred nights to cheer and groan
as Father swore and chipped the plaster,
a game he never cared to master.
My father had his principles.
He smacked to stun them, not to kill.

Frozen underneath the sheets,
I heard the bats mew when he hit.
I heard them drop like squashing fruit.
I heard him test them with his foot.
I knew when he unlatched the screen
and sent them skimming by one wing.

The fall revived them, so he said.
I cried. I wished that they were dead.
I begged him stuff the chimney stack.
I pinched my lips to stay awake
to keep those flapping rats outside,
sang to myself, told riddles, prayed.

I memorized those crepey nights
with dying fireflies for lights:
the heave of wings come down horn-mad
to thump and thwack against the shade.
No matter that my parents said
it only happened twice that way

and all the rest were in my head.
Once, before my father died,
I meant to ask him why he chose
to loose those furies at my bed.

On Being Asked to Write a Poem for the Centenary of the Civil War

Good friend, from my province what is there to say?
My great-grandfather left me here
rooted in grateful guilt,
who came, an escaped conscript
blasted out of Europe in 1848;
came, mourned by all his kin
who put on praying hats
and sat a week on footstools there;
plowed forty days by schooner
and sailed in at Baltimore
a Jew, and poor;
strapped needles up and notions
and walked packaback across
the dwindling Alleghenies,
his red beard and nutmeg freckles
dusting as he sang.

There are no abolitionists in my past to point to.
The truth is that this man,
my only link with that event,
prospered in Virginia, begat
eight young and sewed eight years
on shirts to get them bread.
When those warm states stood up to fight,
the war made him a factory
in a pasture lot where he sat,
my part-time pacifist,
stitching uniforms for the Confederates.

The gray cloth made him rich;
they say he lived to lose it all.
I have only a buckle and a candlestick
left over, like old rhetoric,
from his days
to show how little I belong.
This is the way I remember it was told,
but in a hundred years
all stories go wrong.

The First Rain of Spring

This is the first rain of spring;
it is changing to snow in the west.
The children sleep, closing the ring;
this is the first rain of spring.
Darkly, inside the soft nest,
the children sleep, closing the ring,
It is changing to snow in the west.

We store for death's fattening
the easeful seed in its caul.
It clasps and unclasps like a spring;
we store for death's fattening.
Feel it! The fist to the wall;
it clasps and unclasps like a spring,
mindless, habitual,
the easeful seed in its caul.

Days will expand to the west;
winter is over is all.
Darkly, inside the soft nest,
days will expand to the west.
Feel it! The fist to the wall;
we hoard for life's sweetening.
Winter is over is all.
The children sleep, closing the ring.

from

The Privilege

Morning Swim

Into my empty head there come
a cotton beach, a dock wherefrom

I set out, oily and nude
through mist, in chilly solitude.

There was no line, no roof or floor
to tell the water from the air.

Night fog thick as terry cloth
closed me in its fuzzy growth.

I hung my bathrobe on two pegs.
I took the lake between my legs.

Invaded and invader, I
went overhand on that flat sky.

Fish twitched beneath me, quick and tame.
In their green zone they sang my name

and in the rhythm of the swim
I hummed a two-four-time slow hymn.

I hummed "Abide With Me." The beat
rose in the fine thrash of my feet,

rose in the bubbles I put out
slantwise, trailing through my mouth.

My bones drank water; water fell
through all my doors. I was the well

that fed the lake that met my sea
in which I sang "Abide With Me."

Sisyphus

When I was young and full of shame
I knew a legless man who came

inside a little cart, inchmeal,
flatirons on his hands, downhill.

Under the railroad bridge his chant
singsonged all day *repent, repent*

for Jesus. On the way to school
I spoke to him to save my soul

and coming back, he made me stop
to count the nickels in his cap.

Eyes level with my petticoat
he whined to me. I smelled his goat-

smell, randy, thick, as brown as blood.
I did the only thing I could.

I wheeled my master up the hill.
I rolled him up as he sat still.

Up past the sisters of Saint Joe
I pushed my stone so God would know.

And he, who could not genuflect
on seamy stumps, stitched his respect

with fingers in the air. He called
me a perfect Christian child.

One day I said I was a Jew.
I wished I had. I wanted to.

The basket man is gone; the stone
I push uphill is all my own.

The Pawnbroker

The symbol inside this poem is my father's feet
which, after fifty years of standing behind
the counter waiting on trade,
were tender and smooth and lay on the ironed sheet,
a study of white on white, like a dandy's shirt.
A little too precious; custom-made.
At the end of a day and all day Sunday they hurt.
Lying down, they were on his mind.

The sight of his children barefoot gave him a pain
—part anger, part wonder—as sharp as gravel
inside his lisle socks.
Polacks! he said, but meant it to mean
hod carriers, greenhorns, peasants; not ghetto Poles
once removed. *Where are your shoes? In hock?*
I grew up under the sign of those three gold balls
turning clockwise on their swivel.

Every good thing in my life was secondhand.
It smelled of having been owned before me by
a redcap porter whose ticket
ran out. I saw his time slip down like sand
in the glass that measured our breakfast eggs. At night
he overtook me in the thicket
and held me down and beat my black heart white
to make the pawnbroker's daughter pay.

On Saturday nights the lights stayed lit until ten.
There were cops outside on regular duty to let

the customers in and out.
I have said that my father's feet were graceful and clean.
They hurt when he turned the lock
on the cooks and chauffeurs and unlucky racetrack touts
and carwash attendants and laundresses and stock-
room boys and doormen in epaulets;

they hurt when he did up accounts in his head
at the bathroom sink
of the watches, cameras, typewriters, suitcases, guitars,
cheap diamond rings and thoroughbred
family silver, and matched them against the list
of hot goods from Headquarters,
meanwhile nailbrushing his knuckles and wrists
clean of the pawn-ticket stains of purple ink.

Firsthand I had from my father a love ingrown
tight as an oyster, and returned it
as secretly. From him firsthand
the grace of work, the sweat of it, the bone-
tired unfolding down from stress.
I was the bearer he paid up on demand
with one small pearl of selfhood. Portionless,
I am oystering still to earn it.

Not of the House of Rothschild, my father, my creditor
lay dead while they shaved his cheeks and blacked his mustache.
My lifetime appraiser, my first prince whom death unhorsed
lay soberly dressed and barefoot to be burned.
That night, my brothers and I forced
the cap on his bottle of twenty-year-old Scotch
and drank ourselves on fire beforehand
for the sacrament of closing down the hatch,

for the sacrament of easing down the ways
my thumb-licking peeler of cash on receipt of the merchandise,
possessor of miracles left unredeemed on the shelf
after thirty days,
giver and lender, no longer in hock to himself,
ruled off the balance sheet,
a man of great personal order
and small white feet.

The Appointment

This is my wolf. He sits
at the foot of the bed
in the dark all night

breathing so evenly
I am almost deceived.
It is not the swollen

cat uncurling
restlessly, a house
of kittens knocking

against her flanks;
it isn't the hot fog
fingering the window locks

while the daffodils
wait in the wings
like spearholders;

not the children fisted
in three busy dreams
they will retell at breakfast;

and not you, clearly
not you beside me
all these good years

that he watches.
I lie to him nightlong.
I delay him with praises.

In the morning we wash
together chummily.
I rinse my toothbrush.

After that,
he puts his red eyes out
under the extra blanket.

Quarry, Pigeon Cove

The dead city waited,
hung upside down in the quarry
without leafmold or pondweed
or a flurry of transparent minnows.
Badlands the color of doeskin
lay open like ancient Egypt.

Frog fins strapped to my feet,
a teaspoon of my own spit in the mask
to keep the glass from fogging,
and the thumbsuck rubber air tube in my mouth,
I slid in on my stomach,
a makeshift amphibian.

Whatever the sky was doing
it did now on its own.
The sun shone for the first fifteen feet going down,
then flattened, then petered out.
I hung on the last rung of daylight,
breathing out silver ball bearings,
and looked for the square granite bottom.

I might have swum down looking
soundlessly into nothing,
down stairways and alleys of nothing
until the city took notice
and made me its citizen,
except that life stirred overhead.
I looked up. A dog walked over me.

A dog was swimming and splashing.
Air eggs nested in his fur.
The hairless parts of him bobbled like toys
and the silk of his tail blew past like milkweed.
The licorice pads of his paws
sucked in and out,
making the shapes of kisses.

After that,
the nap of the surface resettled.
Mites danced on both sides of it.
Coming up, my own face seemed beautiful.
The sun broke on my back.

Prothalamion

The far court opens for us all July.
Your arm, flung up like an easy sail bellying,
comes down on the serve in a blue piece of sky
barely within reach, and you following
tip forward on the smash. The sun sits still
on the hard white linen lip of the net. Five-love.
Salt runs behind my ears at thirty-all.
At game I see the sweat that you're made of.
We improve each other, quickening so by noon
that the white game moves itself, the universe
contracted to the edge of the dividing line
you toe against, limbering for your service,
arm up, swiping the sun time after time,
and the square I live in, measured out with lime.

Purgatory

And suppose the darlings get to Mantua,
suppose they cheat the crypt, what next? Begin
with him, unshaven. Though not, I grant you, a
displeasing cockerel, there's egg yolk on his chin.
His seedy robe's aflap, he's got the rheum.
Poor dear, the cooking lard has smoked her eye.
Another Montague is in the womb
although the first babe's bottom's not yet dry.
She scrolls a weekly letter to her Nurse
who dares to send a smock through Balthasar,
and once a month, his father posts a purse.
News from Verona? Always news of war.
  Such sour years it takes to right this wrong!
  The fifth act runs unconscionably long.

from Joppa Diary

January 25th

All night in the flue like a trapped thing,
like a broken bird,
the wind knocked unanswered.
Snow fell down the chimney, making
the forked logs spit
ashes of resurrected crickets.
By 3 a.m. both stoves were dead.
A ball of steel wool
froze to the kitchen window sill,
while we lay back to back in bed,

two thin survivors. Somewhere in a small dream,
a chipmunk uncorked from his hole
and dodged along the wall.
My love, we live at such extremes
that when, in the leftover spite of the storm,
we touch and grow warm,
I can believe I saw
the ground release
that brown and orange commonplace
sign of thaw.

Now daylight the color of buttermilk
tunnels through the coated glass.
Lie still; lie close.
Watch the sun pick
splinters from the window flowers.

Now under the ice, under twelve knee-deep layers
of mud in last summer's pond
the packed hearts of peepers are beating
barely, barely repeating
themselves enough to hang on.

MAY 10TH

I mean
the fiddleheads have forced their babies,
blind topknots first, up from the thinking rhizomes
and the shrew's children, twenty to a teaspoon,
breathe to their own astonishment
in the peephole burrow.

I mean
a new bat hangs upside down in the privy;
its eyes are stuck tight, its wrinkled pink mouth twitches
and in the pond, itself an invented puddle,
tadpoles quake from the jello
and come into being.

I mean, walk softly.
The maple's little used-up bells are dropping
and the new leaves are now unpacking,
still wearing their dimestore lacquer,
still cramped and wet from the journey.

JUNE 15TH

On this day of errors
a field mouse brings forth her young
in my desk drawer.

Come for a pencil,
I see each one,
a wet steel thimble pulled out of its case,
begin to worm its way uphill
to a pinhead teat.

As if I were an enlarged owl
made both gross and cruel,
I lean closer.

The mother rears and kills.
Her forelegs loop like paper clips
as she tears at her belly fur,
shredding it fine as onion skin,
biting the blind and voiceless nubbles off.

Later, she runs past me.
I see her mouth
is stuffed full of a dead baby.

SEPTEMBER 22ND

for Q. on the high seas

Reading late,
last-awake in the country,
I think I hear burned babies screaming,
screaming in the basswood by my window.
I am slow to grow used to owl talk,
slow to let it fall unquestioned
between the lines
but somewhere past midnight
can hear in the spaces

the small mayday alarms of chilled cicadas.
They are almost done.
No sleepier, I create my fear
for a diversion.

Where you are,
the long swells, secret as lava,
take the *France* and bear her
off to Le Havre.
We have our own constants.
There is a world of water between us
and the humpbacks of these
mink hills between us
and three months before we will speak
except in the mechanical click
that our portables make
talking on onionskin
across the Atlantic.

All August I leased the basswood
to a beehive as loud as an airfield.
They sucked and bottled until
the last pods scattered over Joppa.
For two weeks together
we tapped the keys of the city;
its brass doorknobs grew greasy
from our hand turns,
its pavements went hollow
under our footfalls,
everything turned dark with use.
At that time we were careful to say nothing—
we had time, that old excuse.

Now I am
in the country of the no-see-ums,
those midges finer than any netting
that blot the bedsheets all night long.
I am reminded by their little poisons
that something is going on:
up the dirt road, two deer click in the quiet.
Porcupines chew on the willows.
A raccoon taps into my ashcan
and trails off to wash
the eyes from a sour potato.

Darling, what are your noises?
Downstairs from you, great turbines
force the ship's blind screw
to roll in its socket.
Barnacles ride unbending
on the plate of the hull.
Do you dance, play shuffleboard,
bet on the ship's pool?
Have you selected your lifeboat?
Are you on deck at landfall?
Who speaks in your dreams?

There are bat-size dusty millers at my screen.
They will overtake me if I look.
I hear the thud and bump of their longings
imitate the machinery of love.
Let me squash ten of them
and no blood will run.
Inside, they are powder,
a damp and grainy sawdust.
Inside, I am flamboyantly red,

warm, bare; as warm
as the bare bulb that lights my book.

My darling,
the leaves of the fire thorn tree
gave way in last night's rain
and a nest came to light this morning
knitted around five thorns,
its orifice so cunningly made
no predator could enter.
A pear-shaped nest,
an empty pocketbook,
an empty womb
still lined with her white breast fur.

I am tired of this history of loss!
What drum can I beat to reach you?
To be reasonable
is to put out the light.
To be reasonable is to let go.
The eye of the moon is as bland
as new butter. There is no other light
to wink at or salute.
Now let the loudest sound I send you
be the fuzzheads of ripe butternuts
dropping tonight in Joppa like
the yellow oval tears of some rare dinosaur,
dropping to build up
the late September ground.

from

The Nightmare Factory

The Presence

Something went crabwise
across the snow this morning.
Something went hard and slow
over our hayfield.
It could have been a raccoon
lugging a knapsack,
it could have been a porcupine
carrying a tennis racket,
it could have been something
supple as a red fox
dragging the squawk and spatter
of a crippled woodcock.
Ten knuckles underground
those bones are seeds now
pure as baby teeth
lined up in the burrow.

I cross on snowshoes
cunningly woven from
the skin and sinews of
something else that went before.

The Vealers

They come forth with all four legs folded in
like a dimestore card table.
Their hides are watered silk.
As in blindman's buff they rise, unable
to know except by touch, and begin
to root from side to side in search of milk.

The stanchions hang empty. Straw beds the planks
that day. On that day they are left at will
to nuzzle and malinger
under the umbrella of their mothers' flanks
sucking from those four fingers
they were called forth to fill.

Immediately thereafter each is penned
narrowly and well, like a Strasbourg goose.
Milk comes on schedule in a nippled pail.
It is never enough to set them loose
from that birthday dividend
of touch. Bleating racks the jail.

Across the barn the freshened cows
answer until they forget who is there.
Morning and night, machinery
empties their udders. Grazing allows
them to refill. The hungry
calves bawl and doze sucking air.

The sponges of their muzzles pucker
and grow wet with nursing dreams.
In ten weeks' time the knacker
—the local slaughterer—will back his truck
against the ramp, and prodded to extremes
they will kick and buck

and enter
and in our time they will come forth for good
dead center
wrapped and labeled in a plastic sheet,
their perfect flesh unstreaked with blood
or muscle, and we will eat.

Watering Trough

Let the end of all bathtubs
be this putting out to pasture
of four Victorian bowlegs
anchored in grasses.

Let all longnecked browsers
come drink from the shallows
while faucets grow rusty
and porcelain yellows.

Where once our nude forebears
soaped up in this vessel
come, cows, and come, horses.
Bring burdock and thistle,

come slaver the scum of
timothy and clover
on the cast-iron lip that
our grandsires climbed over

and let there be always
green water for sipping
that muzzles may enter thoughtful
and rise dripping.

Hello, Hello Henry

My neighbor in the country, Henry Manley,
with a washpot warming on his woodstove,
with a heifer and two goats and yearly chickens,
has outlasted Stalin, Roosevelt and Churchill
but something's stirring in him in his dotage.

Last fall he dug a hole and moved his privy
and a year ago in April reamed his well out.
When the country sent a truck and poles and cable,
his daddy ran the linemen off with birdshot
and swore he'd die by oil lamp, and did.

Now you tell me that all yesterday in Boston
you set your city phone at mine, and had it ringing
inside a dead apartment for three hours
room after empty room, to keep yours busy.
I hear it in my head, that ranting summons.

That must have been about the time that Henry
walked up two miles, shy as a girl come calling,
to tell me he has a phone now, 264, ring two.
It rang one time last week—wrong number.
He'd be pleased if one day I would think to call him.

Hello, hello Henry? Is that you?

Making the Jam without You

for Judy

Old daughter, small traveler
asleep in a German featherbed
under the eaves in a postcard town
of turrets and towers,
I am putting a dream in your head.

Listen! Here it is afternoon.
The rain comes down like bullets.
I stand in the kitchen,
that harem of good smells
where we have bumped hips and
cracked the cupboards with our talk
while the stove top danced with pots
and it was not clear who did
the mothering. Now I am
crushing blackberries
to make the annual jam
in a white cocoon of steam.

Take it, my sleeper. Redo it
in any of your three
languages and nineteen years.
Change the geography.
Let there be a mountain,
the fat cows on it belled
like a cathedral. Let
there be someone beside you
as you come upon the ruins

of a schloss, all overgrown
with a glorious thicket,
its brambles soft as wool.
Let him bring the buckets
crooked on his angel arms
and may the berries, vaster
than any forage in
the mild hills of New Hampshire,
drop in your pail, plum-size,
heavy as the eyes
of an honest dog
and may you bear them
home together to a square
white unreconstructed kitchen
not unlike this one.

Now may your two heads
touch over the kettle,
over the blood of the berries
that drink up sugar and sun,
over that tar-thick boil
love cannot stir down.
More plainly than
the bric-a-brac of shelves
filling with jelly glasses,
more surely than
the light driving through them
trite as rubies, I see him
as pale as paraffin beside you.
I see you cutting
fresh baked bread to spread it
with the bright royal fur.

At this time
I lift the flap of your dream
and slip out thinner than a sliver
as your two mouths open
for the sweet stain of purple.

For My Great-Grandfather: A Message Long Overdue

You with the beard as red as Barbarossa's
uncut from its first sprouting to the hour
they tucked it in your belt and closed your eyes,
you with the bright brass water pipe, a surefire
plaything under the neighbors' children's noses
for you to puff and them to idolize

—the pipe you'd packed up out of somewhere
in Bohemia, along with the praying shawl
and the pair of little leather praying boxes—
Great-Grandfather, old blue-eyed fox of foxes,
I have three pages of you. That is all.

1895. A three-page letter
from Newport News, Virginia, written
on your bleached-out bills of sale under the stern
heading: ROSENBERG THE TAILOR, DEBTOR,
A FULL LINE OF GOODS OF ALL THE LATEST IN
SUITING AND PANTS. My mother has just been born.

You write to thank your daughter for the picture
of that sixth grandchild. There are six more to come.
"My heart's tenderest tendrils" is your style.
"God bless you even as He blessed Jacob." Meanwhile
you stitch the year away in Christendom.

Meanwhile it seems you've lost your wife, remarried
a girl your daughter's age and caused distress.
"It was a cold relentless hand of Death

that scattered us abroad," you write, "robbing us
of Wife and Mother." Grieving for that one buried
you send new wedding pictures now herewith
and close with *mazel* and *brocha*, words that bless.

The second bride lived on in one long study
of pleats and puckers to the age of ninety-two,
smoked cigarettes, crocheted and spoke of you
to keep our kinship threaded up and tidy.

Was that the message—the erratic ways
the little lore that has been handed on
suffers, but sticks it out in the translation?
I tell you to my children, who forget,
are brimful of themselves, and anyway
might have preferred a farmer or a sailor,
but you and I are buttoned, flap to pocket.
Welcome, ancestor, Rosenberg the Tailor!
I choose to be a lifetime in your debt.

We Are

Love, we are a small pond.
In us yellow frogs take the sun.
Their legs hang down. Their thighs open
like the legs of the littlest children.
On our skin waterbugs suggest incision
but leave no marks of their strokes.
Touching is like that. And what touch evokes.

Just here the blackest berries fatten
over the pond of our being.
It is a rich month for putting up weeds.
They jut like the jaws of Hapsburg kings.
Tomorrow they will drop their blood
as the milkweed bursts its cotton
leaving dry thorns and tight seeds.

Meanwhile even knowing
that time comes down to shut the door
—headstrong, righteous, time hard at the bone
with ice and one thing more—
we teem, we overgrow. The shelf
is tropic still. Even knowing
that none of us can catch up with himself

we are making a run
for it. Love, we are making a run.

After Love

Afterward, the compromise.
Bodies resume their boundaries.

These legs, for instance, mine.
Your arms take you back in.

Spoons of our fingers, lips
admit their ownership.

The bedding yawns, a door
blows aimlessly ajar

and overhead, a plane
singsongs coming down.

Nothing is changed, except
there was a moment when

the wolf, the mongering wolf
who stands outside the self

lay lightly down, and slept.

The Nightmare Factory

these are the dream machines
the dream machines
they put black ants in your bed
silverfish in your ears
they raise your father's corpse
they stick his bones in your sleep
or his stem or all thirty-two
of his stainless steel teeth
they line them up
like the best orchestra seats

these are the nightmare tools
down the assembly line
they send an ocean of feces
you swim in and wake from
with blood on your tongue
they build blind sockets
of subways and mine pits
for you to stop in
the walls slick as laundry soap
swelling and shrinking

these are the presses
they hum in nine languages
sing to the orphans
who eat pins for supper
the whole map of europe
hears the computers click
shunting the trains you take

onto dead sidings
under a sky that is
packed full of blackbirds

night after night in
the bowels of good citizens
nazis and cossacks ride
klansmen and judases
postmen with babies
stuffed in their mailsacks
and for east asians
battalions of giants
dressed in g i fatigues
ears full of bayonets

here on the drawing board
fingers and noses
leak from the air brush
maggots lie under
if i should die before
if i should die
in the back room
stacked up in smooth boxes
like soapflakes or tunafish
wait the undreamt of

from

Up Country

The Hermit Wakes to Bird Sounds

He startles awake. His eyes are full of white light.
In a minute the sun will ooze into the sky.
Meanwhile, all the machines of morning start up.

The typewriter bird is at it again.
Her style is full of endearing hesitations.
The words, when they come, do so in
the staccato rush of a deceitful loveletter.

The sewing machine bird returns to the doddering elm.
Like Penelope, she rips out yesterday's stitches
only to glide up and down, front and back
reentering the same needle holes.

The bird who presides at the wellhouse primes the pump.
Two gurgles, a pause, four squeaks of the handle
and time after time a promise of water
can be heard falling back in the pipe's throat.

Far off the logging birds saw into heartwood
with rusty blades, and the grouse cranks up
his eternally unstartable Model T
and the oilcan bird comes with his liquid pock pock

to attend to the flinty clanks of the disparate parts
and as the old bleached sun slips into position
slowly the teasing inept malfunctioning
one-of-a-kind machines fall silent.

The Hermit Meets the Skunk

The hermit's dog skitters home
drunk with it once every fall,
the whites of his eyes marbled
from the spray and his tail tucked
tighter than a clamshell. He contracts
himself to a mouse under the hermit's bed.

The hermit unsticks him with a broom
and ties him outside to a tree.
He is a spotted dog, black rampant
on white. And as the hermit scrubs,
the white goes satiny with Lava soap,
the black brightens to a bootblack shine.
Next, a dose of tomato juice stains
the white like a razor cut under water
and purples the black, and after that
the whole dog bleaches moon-colored
under a drench of cornstarch.
The hermit sniffs him. Skunk
is still plain as a train announcement.

So he is to be washed again,
rinsed again, powdered again
until the spots wink out again
under the neutral white.
Inside his mouth, the hermit knows
and knows from what is visible
under the tail, Dog is equally spotted
but in the interior, gray on a pink field.

If he were to be pinned down,
his four legs held at four corners,
and slit open by the enthusiast,
the hermit knows the true nature of Dog
spotted layer by layer
would be laid bare.

Afterward all night
skunk sleepwalks the house.
Skunk is a pot of copper pennies
scorched dry on a high flame.
Skunk is a porridge of dead shrews
stewed down to gelatin.
Skunk is the bloat of chicken gut
left ten days to sweeten in the sun.
Skunk is the mother bed, the ripe taste
of carrion, the green kiss.

The Hermit Prays

I hold in my hand this cup
this ritual, this slice of womb
woven of birchbark strips
and the woolly part of a burst cocoon
all mortared with mud and chinked
with papers of snakeskin.

I hold in my hand this carcass
this wintered-over thing.

What they are made of, these string
sacks, these tweezered and gluey cells
can only be said of a house,
of plumb bobs and carpenters' awls.

God of the topmost branch
god of the sheltering leaf
fold your wing over.
Keep secret and keep safe.

The Hermit Picks Berries

At midday the birds doze.
So does he.

The frogs cover themselves.
So does he.

The breeze holds its breath in the poplars.
Not one leaf turns its back.
He admires the stillness.

The snake uncoils its clay self
in the sun on a rock in the pasture.
It is the hermit's pasture.
He encourages the snake.

At this hour a goodly number
of blueberries decide to ripen.
Once they were wax white.
Then came the green of small bruises.
After that, the red of bad welts.
All this time they enlarged themselves.
Now they are true blue.

The hermit whistles as he picks.
Later he will put on his shirt
and walk to town for some cream.

Creatures

See here the diving beetle is split
flat on the underside like a peachpit

and kindergarten blue the frail
biplanes of dragonflies touch head to tail

and water measurers on jury-rigged
legs dent the surface film and whirligigs

crowblack and paddlefooted spin clock-
wise and counter somehow locked

in circus circles and backswimmers all
trim as college racing shells

row trailing their four eyes upside down
and mayflies seek the undersides of stones

to squirt their eggs in rows as straight as corn
and only after clamber out to drown

and the pond's stillness nippled as if
by rain instead is pocked with life

and all, all except the black horseleech
let pass my entering pale enormous flesh.

Stones

The moving of stones, that sly jockeying thrust
takes place at night underground, shoulders first.

They bud in their bunkers like hydras. They puff
up head after head and allow them to drop off

on their own making quahogs, cow flops, eggs and knee
caps. In this way one stone can infuse a colony.

Eyeless and unsurprised they behave
in the manner of stones: swallow turnips, heave graves

rise up openmouthed into walls and from time
to time imitate oysters or mushrooms.

The doors of my house are held open by stones
and to see the tame herd of them hump their backbones

as cumbrous as bears across the pasture in
an allday rain is to believe for an afternoon

of objects that waver and blur
in some dark obedient order.

The Dreamer, the Dream

After the sleeper has burst his night pod
climbed up out of its silky holdings
the dream must stumble alone now
must mope in the hard eye of morning

in search of some phantom outcome
while on both sides of the tissue
the dreamer walks into the weather
past time in September woods in the rain

where the butternuts settle around him
louder than tears and in fact he comes
upon great clusters of honey mushrooms
breaking the heart of old oak

a hundred caps grotesquely piggyback
on one another, a caramel mountain
all powdered with their white spores
printing themselves in no notebook

and all this they do in secret
climbing behind his back
lumbering from their dark fissure
going up like a dream going on.

Beans

. . . making the earth say beans instead of grass—this was my daily work.

—*Thoreau,* Walden

Having planted
that seven-mile plot
he came to love it
more than he had wanted.
His own sweat
sweetened it.
Standing pat
on his shadow
hoeing every noon
it came to pass
in a summer long gone
that Thoreau
made the earth say beans
instead of grass.

You, my gardener
setting foot
among the weeds
that stubbornly reroot
have raised me up
into hellos
expansive as
those everbearing rows.

Even without
the keepsake strings
to hold the shoots

of growing things
I know this much:
I say beans
at your touch.

Mud

You would think that the little birches
would die of that brown mouth sucking
and sucking their root ends.
The rain runs yellow.
The mother pumps in, pumps in
more than she can swallow.
All of her pockmarks spill over.
The least footfall
brings up rich swill.

The streams grow sick with their tidbits.
The trout turn up their long bellies.
The slugs come alive. An army
of lips works in its own ocean.
The boulders gape to deliver themselves.
Stones will be born of that effort.

Meanwhile the mother is sucking.
Pods will startle apart,
pellets be seized with a fever
and as the dark gruel thickens,
life will stick up a finger.

Woodchucks

Gassing the woodchucks didn't turn out right.
The knockout bomb from the Feed and Grain Exchange
was featured as merciful, quick at the bone
and the case we had against them was airtight,
both exits shoehorned shut with puddingstone,
but they had a sub-sub-basement out of range.

Next morning they turned up again, no worse
for the cyanide than we for our cigarettes
and state-store Scotch, all of us up to scratch.
They brought down the marigolds as a matter of course
and then took over the vegetable patch
nipping the broccoli shoots, beheading the carrots.

The food from our mouths, I said, righteously thrilling
to the feel of the .22, the bullets' neat noses.
I, a lapsed pacifist fallen from grace
puffed with Darwinian pieties for killing,
now drew a bead on the littlest woodchuck's face.
He died down in the everbearing roses.

Ten minutes later I dropped the mother. She
flipflopped in the air and fell, her needle teeth
still hooked in a leaf of early Swiss chard.
Another baby next. O one-two-three
the murderer inside me rose up hard,
the hawkeye killer came on stage forthwith.

There's one chuck left. Old wily fellow, he keeps
me cocked and ready day after day after day.
All night I hunt his humped-up form. I dream
I sight along the barrel in my sleep.
If only they'd all consented to die unseen
gassed underground the quiet Nazi way.

from

House, Bridge, Fountain, Gate

History Lesson

for Steven

You were begotten in a vague war.
American planes ran their fingers
through the sky between truces
as your daddy crossed parallels
to plant you as bald as an onion
in 1954.

Two years later you sailed
you think you remember
on a converted troopship full
of new wives and wet pants while
the plum pits of your mother's eyes
wobbled and threatened to come loose.

After that there were knots to undo
in your absent father's GI work boots
and the sounds of night robbers
cantering up the staircase
ransacking the rooming house
where you lived with your almond-eyed mother.

When they whisked her away in a bedroll
of lipstick and false eyelashes,
the landlady sent for the cops.
All the way to your first state school
a stoic, age six-and-a-half
you played games with the sergeant's handcuffs.

It is true that we lie down on cowflops
praying they'll turn into pillows.
It is true that our mothers explode
out of the snowballs of dreams
or speak to us down the chimney
saying our names above the wind.

That a man may be free of his ghosts
he must return to them like a garden.
He must put his hands in the sweet rot
uprooting the turnips, washing them
tying them into bundles
and shouldering the whole load to market.

The Thirties Revisited

It starts with the clothes-prop man
who is driving his stickload of notches and points
down the streets of my childhood. His horse
knocks from side to side on Lincoln Log joints
and the feedbag sways at the rear
dribbling its measure of oats.
It's the thirties again, that dream. I'm assigned
to remember laundry lifting like ghosts
on the propped-up lines where step-ins blush,
the cheeks of trousers fill, and skirts
open their petals in the washday wind.
But why just now must the horse go lame,
drop in the shafts and be left behind
struggling, struggling so to rise
that blood pours from his nose?
Why is he shot
on this Monday noon of my queer pinched life
as I watch from the parlor window seat?

Adam and Eve and Pinch Me
went down to the river to bathe.
Adam and Eve got drowneded
and who do you think got saved?

My father's bootlegger has just driven up
from Camden with a case of Cutty Sark
for the demon whiskey lovers.
My uncles move in upstairs with their beebee guns.

They're out of work.
God has a peephole even under the covers.
Squirrels fall at first light out of the pin oaks.
My brothers, short-pants man to man,
tie them in knots like old socks
and salt them away in the garbage can.
I'm the squirrel girl.
After everyone leaves for school or town
I sneak the poor burst darlings down
to the garden bed for a burial.

On the way back, muddy, I stop for a drink
at the kitchen faucet, wash up, hear
the amber bottles whistle through me clear
as scatter shot, then do
what the Almighty tells me to:
I pour my daddy's whiskey down the sink.

Adam and Eve and Pinch Me Tight
went to the movies one dark night.
Adam and Eve had an ice-cream cone
and who do you think got lost coming home?

Now I am ten. Enter Mamselle,
my mother's cut-rate milliner.
She is putting her sore eyes out in the hall
at thirty cents an hour
tacking veils onto felt forms.
Mamselle is an artist.
She can copy the Eiffel Tower
in feathers with a rolled-up brim.
She can make pyramids out of cherries.
Mamselle wears cheese boxes on her feet.

Madame can buy and sell her.
If daughters were traded among the accessories
in the perfumed hush of Bonwit Teller's
she'd have replaced me with a pocketbook,
snapped me shut and looped me over
her Hudson seal cuff; me of the chrome-wire mouth,
the inkpot braids, one eye that looks
wrongly across at the other.
O Lady of the Chaise Longue,
O Queen of the Kimono,
I disappoint my mother.

Adam and Eve and Pinch Me Flat
went to the push-nickel automat.
Adam and Eve had nickels to spend
but who do you think got left in the end?

Two more years of Kaltenborn's reports
and Poland will fall, the hearts
of horses will burst in a battle with tanks.
Soon enough the uncles will give thanks
for GI uniforms to choose
and go off tough as terriers to dig their holes.
Warsaw will excrete its last Jews.

My father will cry like a child.
He will knuckle his eyes, to my terror,
over the letters that come from the grave
begging to be sponsored, plucked up, saved.
I hoard tinfoil, meanwhile.
I knit for Britain's warriors.
This is the year that my mother stiffens.
She undresses in the closet giving me

her back as if I can't see
her breasts fall down like pufferfish,
the life gone out of their crusty eyes.
But who has punctured the bathroom light?
Why does the mattress moan at night
and why is nothing good
said of all the business to come
—the elastic belt with its metal tongue—
when my body, that surprise,
claps me into my first blood?

Adam and Eve and Pinch Me Dead
coasted down Strawberry Hill on a sled.
Adam and Eve fell off in the mud
but who do you think got covered with blood?

Sperm

You have to admire the workmanship of cousins.
There is a look in our eyes.
Once we were all seventeen of us naked as almonds.
We were all suckled except for Richard
who had to be raised on a glue of bananas.
Now he is bald and breathes through the nose
like an air conditioner but he too
said goodnight, Grandfather, when
we were all sheep in the nursery.
All of those kisses like polka dots
touched to the old man's wrinkles
while his face jittered under our little wet mouths
and he floated to the top of his palsy
sorting out Jacob from Esau.

O Grandfather, look what your seed has done!
Look what has come of those winter night gallops.
You tucking the little wife up
under the comforter that always leaked feathers.
You coming perhaps just as the trolley
derailed taking the corner at 15th Street
in a shower of blue sparks, and Grandmother's
corset spread out like a filleted fish
to air meanwhile on the windowsill.
Each time a secret flourished under those laces
she eased the bones from their moorings
and swelled like the Sunday choir.
Seven sons, all with a certain
shy hood to the eye. I call it the Hummel effect.

But here, in the next generation,
I'm waiting in line at the Sedgwick
with Hester and Laura to see
Our Gang and a Shirley Temple special.
The Sedgwick has stars on the ceiling
and Shirley has banana curls.
If you have to go to the Ladies
Hester says to sit in the air
or else you will catch something awful
Hester says, even a baby.
It is Saturday. I come out in the sun
with a guilty headache while down the street
at the Lutheran Home for Incurable Orphans
a girl my age wet the bed
and stands draped in the sheets to be punished
and she could have been me.
In three years Laura will wake with
a headache that walks down her neck stem
and puts her into a wheelchair.
She grows patient as an animal.
After that I prefer not to know her.

After that, as important as summer,
the southern branch comes north to visit.
There's Sissy and Clara and Rosie
jiggling on pogo sticks, jiggling
in identical pink under-vests
while Nigger, their loyal Labrador
goes after hoptoads in the garden.
I see a brown stain on Sissy's petticoat.
I see that smart aleck, Teddy
playing games behind the furnace
with Clara. They touch in the coal bin.

He gets ten smacks with the hairbrush
and his plane goes down in the Aleutians.
Arthur's still sucking his thumb,
the same arm he loses in Italy.
Meanwhile Frederick and Ben
are born and done up in nappies.
When Frederick is sponged in the basin
and laughs, according to Rosie,
even his little beard wiggles.
Ben buttons up in the Navy
and comes home with five darling ribbons.

Such darlings, those wicked good boys
all but one come to their manhood:
Bo palming poker chips in the frat house,
Joseph gone broody with bourbon,
Michael following the horses
while nursing an early heart murmur,
Alan surprised at the Bide-A-Wee
with an upstate minister's daughter
and diffident James in the closet
trying on Sukey's garter belt,
pulling on Sukey's stockings.

O Grandfather, what is it saying,
these seventeen cousins-german
descending the same number of steps
their chromosomes tight as a chain gang
their genes like innocent porters
a milk churn of spermatozoa?
You have to admire the product—
bringing forth sons to be patriots
daughters to dance like tame puppets—

half of them dead or not speaking
while Sukey and James, the end of the line,
keep house in the gentlest tradition
of spinster and bachelor sweetheart.
Memory dances me backward,
back to your dining room table
added onto to cross the front hall.
It's a squeeze play of damask on damask.
We're all wearing your hooded eyes
as you ask your aphasic blessing
over thirty-two spoons for the pudding.

The Deaths of the Uncles

I am going backward in a home movie.
The reel stutters and balks before it takes hold
but surely these are my uncles spiking the lemonade
and fanning their girls on my grandmother's veranda.
My uncles, innocent of their deaths, swatting
the shuttlecock's white tit in the Sunday twilight.
Some are wearing gray suede spats, the buttons
glint like money. Two are in checkered knickers,
the bachelor uncle in his World War One puttees
is making a mule jump for the cavalry, he is crying
Tuck, damn you, Rastus, you son of a sea cook!
How full of family feeling they are, their seven
bald heads coming back as shiny as an infection,
coming back to testify like Charlie Chaplin,
falling down a lot like Laurel and Hardy.
Stanley a skeleton rattling his closet knob
long before he toppled three flights with Parkinson's.
Everyone knew Miss Pris whom he kept in rooms
over the movie theater, rooms full of rose water
while his wife lay alone at home like a tarnished spoon.
Mitchell the specialist, big bellied, heavy of nose,
broad as a rowboat, sniffed out the spices.
Shrank to a toothpick after his heart attack,
fasted on cottage cheese, threw out his black cigars
and taken at naptime died in his dressing gown
tidy in paisley wool, old pauper thumb in his mouth.
Jasper, the freckled, the Pepsodent smiler,
cuckold and debtor, ten years a deacon
stalled his Pierce Arrow smack on a railroad track

while the twins in their pram cried for a new father.
The twins in their pram as speechless as puppies.
O run the film forward past Lawrence the baby,
the masterpiece, handsomest, favorite issue.
Cover the screen while the hats at his funeral
bob past like sailboats, like black iron cooking pots.
Larry the Lightheart dead of a bullet.
And pass over Horace, who never embezzled,
moderate Horace with sand in his eyelids
so we can have Roger again, the mule trainer
crying *son of a sea cook!* into his dotage,
wearing the Stars and Stripes next to his hearing aid,
shining his Mason's ring, fingering his Shriner's pin,
Roger the celibate, warrior, joiner

but it was Dan Dan Dan the apple of my girlhood
with his backyard telescope swallowing the stars,
with the reedy keening of his B-flat licorice stick,
Dan who took me teadancing at the Adelphia Club.
Dan who took me boating on the Schuylkill scum.
Dan who sent the roses, the old singing telegrams
and cracked apart at Normandy leaving behind
a slow-motion clip of him leading the conga line,
his white bucks in the closet and a sweet worm in my heart.

Life's Work

Mother my good girl
I remember this old story:
you fresh out of the Conservatory
at eighteen a Bach specialist
in a starched shirtwaist
begging permission to go on tour
with the nimble violinist you were
never to accompany and he
flinging his music down
the rosin from his bow
flaking line by line
like grace notes on the treble clef
and my grandfather
that estimable man I never met
scrubbing your mouth with a handkerchief
saying no daughter of mine
tearing loose the gold locket
you wore with no one's picture in it
and the whole German house on 15th Street
at righteous whiteheat. . . .

At eighteen I chose to be a swimmer.
My long hair dripped through dinner
onto the china plate.
My fingers wrinkled like Sunsweet
yellow raisins from the afternoon workout.
My mouth chewed but I was doing laps.
I entered the water like a knife.
I was all muscle and seven doors.

A frog on the turning board.
King of the Eels and the Eel's wife.
I swallowed and prayed
to be allowed to join the Aquacade
and my perfect daddy
who carried you off to elope
after the fingerboard snapped
and the violinist lost his case
my daddy wearing gravy on his face
swore on the carrots and the boiled beef
that I would come to nothing
that I would come to grief. . . .

Well, the firm old fathers are dead
and I didn't come to grief.
I came to words instead
to tell the little tale that's left:
the midnights of my childhood still go on.
The stairs speak again under your foot.
The heavy parlor door folds shut
and "Clair de Lune"
puckers from the obedient keys
plain as a schoolroom clock ticking
and what I hear more clearly than Debussy's
lovesong is the dry aftersound
of your long nails clicking.

The Jesus Infection

Jesus is with me
on the Blue Grass Parkway going eastbound.
He is with me
on the old Harrodsburg Road coming home.
I am listening
to country gospel music
in the borrowed Subaru.
The gas pedal
and the words
leap to the music.
O throw out the lifeline!
Someone is drifting away.

Flags fly up in my mind
without my knowing
where they've been lying furled
and I am happy
living in the sunlight
where Jesus is near.
A man is driving his polled Herefords
across the gleanings of a cornfield
while I am bound for the kingdom of the free.
At the little trestle bridge that has no railing
I see that I won't have to cross Jordan alone.

Signposts every mile exhort me
to Get Right With God
and I move over.
There's a neon message blazing

at the crossroad
catty-corner to the Burger Queen:
Ye Come With Me.
It is well with my soul, Jesus?
It sounds so easy
to be happy after the sunrise,
to be washed in the crimson flood.

Now I am tailgating
and I read a bumper sticker
on a Ford truck full of Poland Chinas.
It says: Honk If You Know Jesus
and I do it.
My sound blats out for miles
behind the pigsqueal
and it's catching in the front end,
in the axle,
in the universal joint,
this rich contagion.

We are going down the valley on a hairpin turn,
the swine and me, we're breakneck in
we're leaning on
the everlasting arms.

Living Alone with Jesus

Can it be
I am the only Jew residing in Danville, Kentucky,
looking for matzoh in the Safeway and the A & P?
The Sears Roebuck salesman wrapping my potato masher
advises me to accept Christ as my personal saviour
or else when I die I'll drop straight down to hell,
but the ladies who come knocking with their pamphlets
say as long as I believe in God that makes us
sisters in Christ. I thank them kindly.

In the county there are thirty-seven churches
and no butcher shop. This could be taken
as a matter of all form and no content.
On the other hand, form can be seen as
an extension of content, I have read that,
up here in the sealed-off wing where my three rooms
are threaded by outdoor steps to the downstairs world.
In the open risers walnut trees are growing.
Sparrows dipped in raspberry juice
come to my one windowsill. Cardinals
are blood spots before my eyes.
My bed is a narrow canoe with a fringy throw.
Whenever I type it takes to the open sea
and comes back wrong end to.
Every morning the pillows produce tapioca.
I gather it up for a future banquet.

I am leading a meatless life. I keep
my garbage in the refrigerator. Eggshells

potato peels and the rinds of cheeses nest
in the empty sockets of my daily grapefruit.
Every afternoon at five I am comforted
by the carillons of the Baptist church next door.
I let the rock of ages cleave for me on Monday.
Tuesday I am washed in the blood of the lamb.
Bringing in the sheaves on Wednesday keeps me busy.
Thursday's the day on Christ the solid rock I stand.
The Lord lifts me up to higher ground on Friday so that
Saturday I put my hands in the nail-scarred hands.
Nevertheless, I stay put on the Sabbath. I let
the whiskey bottle say something scurrilous.

Jesus, if you are in all thirty-seven churches,
are you not also here with me
making it alone in my back rooms like a flagpole sitter
slipping my peanut shells and prune pits into the Kelvinator?
Are you not here at nightfall
ticking in the box of the electric blanket?
Lamb, lamb, let me give you honey on your grapefruit
and toast for the birds to eat
out of your damaged hands.

To Swim, to Believe

Centre College, Danville, Kentucky

The beautiful excess of Jesus on the waters
is with me now in the Boles Natatorium.
This bud of me exults, giving witness:

these flippers that rose up to be arms.
These strings drawn to be fingers.
Legs plumped to make my useful fork.

Each time I tear this seam to enter,
all that I carry is taken from me,
shucked in the dive.

Lovers, children, even words go under.
Matters of dogma spin off in the freestyle
earning that mid-pool spurt, like faith.

Where have I come from? Where am I going?
What do I translate, gliding back and forth
erasing my own stitch marks in this lane?

Christ on the lake was not thinking
where the next heel-toe went.
God did him a dangerous favor

whereas Peter, the thinker, sank.

The secret is in the relenting,
the partnership. I let my body work

accepting the dangerous favor
from this king-size pool of waters.
Together I am supplicant. I am bride.

The Selling of the Slaves

Lexington, Kentucky

The brood mares on the block at Tipton Pavilion
have ears as delicate as wineglass stems.
Their eyes roll up and out like china dolls'.
Dark red petals flutter in their nostrils.
They are a strenuous ballet, the thrust and suck
of those flanks, and meanwhile the bags of foals
joggle, each pushing against its knapsack.

They are brought on one at a time, worked over
in the confines of a chain-link silver tether
by respectful attendants in white jackets
and blackface. The stage manager hovers
in the background with a gleaming shovel
and the air ripens with the droppings he dips up.

In the velvet pews a white-tie congregation
fans itself with the order of the service.
Among them pass the prep-school deacons
in blazers and the emblems of their districts.
Their hymnals are clipboards. The minister
in an Old Testament voice recites
a liturgy of bloodlines. Ladies and Gentlemen:

Hip Number 20 is Rich and Rare
a consistent and highclass producer.
She is now in foal to that good horse, Brazen.
Candy Dish slipped twins on January one
and it is with genuine regret I must announce

that Roundabout, half sister to a champion,
herself a dam of winners, is barren this season.

She is knocked down at eleven thousand dollars
to the man from Paris with a diamond in his tooth,
the man from Paris with a snake eye in his collar.
When money changes hands among men of worth
it is all done with sliding doors and decorum
but snake whips slither behind the curtain.
In the vestry flasks go round. The gavel's
report is a hollow gunshot:
sold, old lady! and the hot
manure of fear perfumes God's chapel.

In the Root Cellar

The parsnips, those rabbis
have braided their beards together
to examine the text. The word
that engrosses them is: February.

To be a green tomato
wrapped in the Sunday book section
is to know nothing. Meanwhile
the wet worm eats his way outward.

These cabbages, these clean keepers
in truth are
a row of impacted stillbirths.
One by one we deliver them.

O potato, a touch of
dankness and you're up with
ten tentative erections.
How they deplete you!

Dusty blue wart hogs, the squash
squat for a thump and a tuning.
If we could iron them out
they'd be patient blue mandolins.

The beets wait wearing their birthmarks.
They will be wheeled into the amphitheater.
Even before the scrub-up, the scalpel,
they bleed a little.

I am perfect, breathes the onion.
I am God's first circle
the tulip that slept in His navel.
Bite me and be born.

The Mummies

Two nights running I was out there
in orange moonlight with old bedsheets
and a stack of summered-over Sunday papers
tucking up the tomatoes while the peppers
whimpered and went under and the radishes
dug in with their dewclaws and all over
the field the goldenrod blackened
and fell down like Napoleon's army.

This morning they're still at it, my tomatoes
making marbles, making more of those little
green volunteers that you can rattle
all winter in a coat pocket, like fingers.
But today on the lip of the solstice
I will pull them, one hundred
big blind greenies. I will stand them
in white rows in the root cellar
wrapped one by one
in the terrible headlines.

Song for Seven Parts of the Body

I.

This one,
a common type,
turns in.
Was once attached.
Fed me as sweetly
as an opium pipe.
O, birthdays unlimber us,
eyes sit back,
ears go indoors,
but here nothing changes.
This was.
This is.

II.

Mostly they lie low
put up shells, sprout hairs
and if they sing, they know
only leather cares.
Blind marchers five abreast
left, right
silent as mushrooms or puff paste
they rise up free at night.

III.

I have a life of my own
he says. He is transformed
without benefit of bone.
I will burrow, he says
and enters. Afterwards
he goes slack as a slug.
He remembers little.
The prince is again a frog.

IV.

Here is a field that never lies fallow.
Sweat waters it, nails hoe the roots.
Every day death comes in with the winnow.
Every day newborns crop up like asparagus.
At night, all night on the pillow
you can hear the narrow sprouts crackle
rubbing against each other,
lying closer than lemmings.
They speak to their outposts in armpits.
They speak to their settlers in crotches.
Neighbor, neighbor, they murmur.

V.

They have eyes that see not.
they straddle the valley of wishes.
Their hills make their own rules.
Among them are bobbers
melons, fishes
doorknobs and spools.
At times they whisper, touch me.

VI.

Imagine a mouth
without you, pink man,
goodfellow.
A house
without a kitchen,
a fishless ocean.
No way to swallow.

VII.

These nubbins
these hangers-on
hear naught.
Wise men
tug them in thought.
Lovers
may nibble each other's.
Maidens
gypsies and peasants
make holes in theirs
to hang presents.

Heaven as Anus

In the Defense Department there is a shop
where scientists sew the eyelids of rabbits open
lest they blink in the scorch of a nuclear drop

and elsewhere dolphins are being taught to defuse
bombs in the mock-up of a harbor and monkeys
learn to perform the simple tasks of draftees.

It is done with electric shocks. Some mice
who have failed their time tests in the maze
now go to the wire unbidden for their jolts.

Implanting electrodes yields rich results:
alley cats turn from predators into prey.
Show them a sparrow and they cower

while the whitewall labs fill up with the feces of fear
where calves whose hearts have been done away
with walk and bleat on plastic pumps.

And what is any of this to the godhead,
these squeals, whines, writhings, unexpected jumps,
whose children burn alive, booby-trap the dead,
lop ears and testicles, core and disembowel?

It all ends at the hole. No words may enter
the house of excrement. We will meet there
as the sphincter of the good Lord opens wide
and He takes us all inside.

Young Nun at Bread Loaf

Sister Elizabeth Michael
has come to the Writers' Conference.
She has white habits like a summer sailor
and a black notebook she climbs into nightly
to sway in the hammock of a hundred knotted poems.
She is the youngest nun I have ever known.

When we go for a walk in the woods
she puts on a dimity apron that teases her boottops.
It is sprigged with blue flowers.
I wear my jeans and sneakers. We are looking
for mushrooms (chanterelles are in season)
to fry and eat with my drinks, her tomato juice.

Wet to the shins with crossing
and recrossing the same glacial brook, a mile
downstream we find them, the little pistols,
denser than bandits among the tree roots.
Forager, she carries the basket.
Her hands are crowded with those tough yellow thumbs.

Hiking back in an unction of our own sweat
she brings up Christ. Christ, that canard!
I grind out a butt and think of the waiting bourbon.
The sun goes down in disappointment.
You can say what you want, she says.
You live as if you believe.

Sister
Sister Elizabeth Michael
says we are doing Christ's work, we two.
She, the rosy girl in a Renoir painting.
I, an old Jew.

Amanda Is Shod

The way the cooked shoes sizzle
dropped in a pail of cold water
the way the coals in the portable forge
die out like hungry eyes
the way the nails go in aslant
each one the tip of a snake's tongue

and the look of the parings
after the farrier's knife
has sliced through.

I collect them
four marbled white C's
as refined as petrified wood
and dry them to circles of bone
and hang them away on my closet hook

lest anyone cast a spell on Amanda.

Amanda Dreams She Has Died and Gone to the Elysian Fields

This morning Amanda
lies down during breakfast.
The hay is hip high.
The sun sleeps on her back
as it did on the spine
of the dinosaur
the fossil bat
the first fish with feet
she was once.
A breeze fans
the deerflies from lighting.
Only a gaggle of gnats
housekeeps in her ears.
A hay plume sticks out of her mouth.

I come calling with a carrot
from which I have taken
the first bite.
She startles
she considers rising
but retracts the pistons
of her legs and accepts
as loose-lipped as a camel.

We sit together.
In this time and place
we are heart and bone.
For an hour
we are incorruptible.

The Agnostic Speaks to Her Horse's Hoof

Come, frog, reveal yourself.
Surface out of the poultice
the muck and manure pack.
Make your miraculous V to stand up.
Show me as well the tickle place
that cleft between.

The Good Book says a man's life
is as grass the wind passes over
and is gone.
According to the *National Geographic*
the oceans will lie down dead
as cesspools in sixty years.

Let us ripen in our own way—
I with my back to the trunk
of a butternut that has caught
the fatal red canker
and on my knee
this skillet of your old foot.

The hoofpick is God's instrument
as much as I know of Him.

In my hands let it raise
your moon, Amanda, your nerve bone.
Let us come to the apocalypse complete

without splinter or stone.
Let us ride out
on four iron feet.

Eyes

At night Amanda's eyes
are rage red with toy worlds inside.
Head on they rummage the dark
of the paddock like twin cigars
but flicker at the edges with
the shyer tongues of the spirit lamp.

There's little enough for her to see:
my white shirt, the sleeves
rolled high, two flaps of stale bread
in my fish paws. I can't sleep.
I have come back from
the feed-bag-checkered restaurant
from the pale loose tears of my dearest friend
her blue eyes sinking into the highball glass
her eyeballs clinking on ice
and her mouth drawn down in the grand
comedy of anguish.

Today a sparrow has been put
in the hawk's hands and in the net
a monarch crazes its wings on gauze.
A doe run down by the dogs
commonly dies of fright before
its jugular opens at the fang hole.
In my friend's eyes, hunger
holds an empty rice bowl.

O Amanda, burn out my dark.
Press the warm suede of your horseflesh
against my cold palm.
Take away all that is human.

Thinking of Death and Dogfood

Amanda, you'll be going
to Alpo or to Gaines
when you run out of luck;
the flesh flensed from your bones
your mammoth rib cage rowing
away to the renderer's
a dry canoe on a truck

while I foresee my corpse
slid feet first into fire
light as the baker's loaf
to make of me at least
a pint of potash spoor.
I'm something to sweeten the crops
when the clock hand stops.

Amanda, us in the woods
miles from home, the ground
upending in yellow flutes
that open but make no sound.
Ferns in the mouth of the brute,
chanterelles in the woman's sack . . .
what do I want for myself
dead center, bareback
on the intricate harp of your spine?
All that I name as mine

with the sure slow oxen of words:
feed sacks as grainy as boards

that air in the sun. A boy
who is wearing my mother's eyes.
Garlic to crush in the pan.
The family gathering in.
Already in the marsh
the yearling maples bleed
a rich onrush. Time slips
another abacus bead.

Let it not stick in the throat
or rattle a pane in the mind.
May I leave no notes behind
wishful, banal or occult
and you, small thinker in
the immensity of your frame,
may you be caught and crammed
midmouthful of the best grain
when the slaughterer's bullet slams
sidelong into your brain.

from

The Retrieval System

The Retrieval System

It begins with my dog, now dead, who all his long life
carried about in his head the brown eyes of my father,
keen, loving, accepting, sorrowful, whatever;
they were Daddy's all right, handed on, except
for their phosphorescent gleam tunneling the night
which I have to concede was a separate gift.

Uncannily when I'm alone these features
come up to link my lost people
with the patient domestic beasts of my life. For example,
the wethered goat who runs free in pasture and stable
with his flecked, agate eyes and his minus-sign pupils
blats in the tiny voice of my former piano teacher

whose bones beat time in my dreams and whose terrible breath
soured "Country Gardens," "Humoresque," and unplayable
  Bach.
My elderly aunts, wearing the heads of willful
intelligent ponies, stand at the fence begging apples.
The sister who died at three has my cat's faint chin,
my cat's inscrutable squint, and cried catlike in pain.

I remember the funeral. *The Lord is my shepherd,*
we said. I don't want to brood. Fact: it is people who fade,
it is animals that retrieve them. A boy
I loved once keeps coming back as my yearling colt,
cocksure at the gallop, racing his shadow
for the hell of it. He runs merely to be.

A boy who was lost in the war thirty years ago
and buried at sea.

Here, it's forty degrees and raining. The weatherman
who looks like my resident owl, the one who goes out and in
by the open haymow, appears on the TV screen.
With his heart-shaped face, he is also my late dentist's double,
donnish, bifocaled, kind. Going a little gray,
advising this wisdom tooth will have to come out someday,
meanwhile filling it as a favor. Another save.
It outlasted him. The forecast is nothing but trouble.
It will snow fiercely enough to fill all these open graves.

The Longing to Be Saved

When the barn catches fire
I am wearing the wrong negligee.
It hangs on me like a gunny sack.
I get the horses out, but they
wrench free, wheel, dash back
and three or four trips are required.
Much whinnying and rearing as well.
This happens whenever I travel.

At the next stopover, the children take off
their doctor and lawyer disguises
and turn back into little lambs.
They cower at windows from which flames
shoot like the tattered red cloth
of dimestore devil suits. They refuse
to jump into my waiting arms, although
I drilled them in this technique, years ago.

Finally they come to their senses and leap
but each time, the hoop holds my mother.
Her skin is as dry and papery
as a late onion. I take her
into my bed, an enormous baby
I do not especially want to keep.
Three nights of such disquiet
in and out of dreams as thin as acetate

until, last of all, it's you
trapped in the blazing fortress.

I hold the rope as you slide from danger.
It's tricky in high winds and drifting snow.
Your body swaying in space
grows heavier, older, stranger

and me in the same gunny sack
and the slamming sounds as the gutted building burns.
Now the family's out, there's no holding back.
I go in to get my turn.

Address to the Angels

Taking off at sunset over the city
it seems we pull the sun up
and pin it over the rim
or is it the other way round,
is it the horizon we push down
like a loose cuticle?
I am up here grieving, tallying
my losses, and I think how once
the world was flat and rested on
the back of a giant fish whose tail
was in his mouth and on the Day
of Judgment all the sinners fell
overboard into the black gulf.
Once, we walked distances
or went by horse and knew our places
on the planet, gravity-wise.

Now angels, God's secret agents,
I am assured by Billy Graham,
circulate among us to tell
the living they are not alone.
On twenty-four-hour duty, angels
flutter around my house and barn
blundering into the cobwebs,
letting pots boil over
or watching the cat torture
a chipmunk. When my pony,
filching apples, rears and catches
his halter on a branch and hangs

himself all afternoon, I like
to think six equine angels fan
the strangling beast
until his agony is past.

Who knows how much or little
anyone suffers? Animals
are honest through their inability
to lie. Man, in his last hour,
has a compulsion to come clean.
Death is the sacred criterion.
Always it is passion that
confuses the issue. Always
I think that no one
can be sadder than I am.
For example, now, watching
this after after-sunset
in the sky on top of Boston
I am wanting part of my life back.
so I can do it over.
So I can do it better.

Angels, where were you when
my best friend did herself in?
Were you lunching beside us
that final noon, did you catch
some nuance that went past my ear?
Did you ease my father out
of his cardiac arrest that wet
fall day I sat at the high crib bed
holding his hand? And when
my black-eyed Susan-child ran
off with her European lover

and has been ever since an unbelonger,
were you whirligiging over
the suitcases? Did you put
your imprimatur on
that death-by-separation?

It's no consolation, angels,
knowing you're around
helplessly observing like
some sacred CIA. Even
if you're up here, flattened
against the Fasten Your Seatbelt sign
or hugging the bowl in the lavatory,
we are, each one of us, our own
prisoner. We are
locked up in our own story.

My Father's Neckties

Last night my color-blind chain-smoking father
who has been dead for fourteen years
stepped up out of a basement tie shop
downtown and did not recognize me.

The number he was wearing was as terrible
as any from my girlhood, a time of
ugly ties and acrimony: six or seven
blue lightning bolts outlined in yellow.

Although this was my home town it was tacky
and unfamiliar, it was Rabat or Gibraltar
Daddy smoking his habitual
square-in-the-mouth cigarette and coughing
ashes down the lightning jags. He was
my age exactly, it was wordless, a window
opening on an interior we both knew
where we had loved each other, keeping it quiet.

Why do I wait years and years to dream this outcome?
My brothers, in whose dreams he must as surely
turn up wearing rep ties or polka dots clumsily
knotted, do not speak of their encounters.

When we die, all four of us, in
whatever sequence, the designs
will fall off like face masks

and the rayon ravel from this hazy version
of a man who wore hard colors recklessly
and hid out in the foreign
bargain basements of his feelings.

Progress Report

The middle age you wouldn't wait
for now falls on me, white
as a caterpillar tent, white
as the sleetfall from apple trees
gone wild, petals that stick
in my hair like confetti
as I cut my way through clouds
of gnats and blackflies in the woods.

The same scarlet tanager
as last year goes up, a red
rag flagging from tree to tree,
lending a rakish permanence to
the idea of going on without you

even though my empty times
still rust like unwashed dogfood cans
and my nights fill up with porcupine
dung he drops on purpose at
the gangway to the aluminum-
flashed willow, saying that
he's been here, saying he'll come
back with his tough waddle, his pig eyes,
saying he'll get me yet. He is
the stand-in killer I use
to notarize your suicide
two years after, in deep spring.

Thomas Mann's permit to take
refuge in Switzerland said:
"for literary activities and
the passage of life's evening."
I wonder if all those he loved
and outlived showed up nights
for chips of reconstructed
dialogue under the calm Alps,
he taking both parts, working it out.
Me taking both parts in what
I suppose is my life's afternoon.

Dear friend, last night I dreamed
you held a sensitive position,
you were Life's Counselor
coming to the phone in Vaud or Bern,
some terse one-syllable place,
to tell me how to carry on

and I woke into the summer solstice
swearing I will break
your absence into crumbs
like the stump of a punky tree
working its way down
in the world's evening
down to the forest floor.

The Food Chain

The Hatchery's old bachelor, Henry Manley
backs his pickup axle-deep into my pond
opens the double tub of brookies
and begins dipping out his fingerlings.
Going in, they glint like chips of mica.

Henry waits a while to see them school up.
They flutter into clumps like living rice grains.
He leaves me some foul-smelling pellets
with instructions how to sow them on the water
a few days until they smarten and spread out.

What *he* does is shoot kingfishers with his air rifle.
They ate two thousand fry on him last weekend.
Herons? They hunt frogs, but watch for martens.
They can clean a pond out overnight.
He stands there, busy with his wrists, and looking savage.

Knowing he knows we'll hook his brookies
once they're a sporting size, I try for something
but all the words stay netted in my mouth.
Henry waves, guns the engine. His wheels spin
then catch.

The Henry Manley Blues

Henry Manley's house, unpainted for
eighty years, shrinks as attached sheds crease
and fold like paper wings. An elm tree shears
the sitting porch off in a winter storm.
And Henry's fields are going under, where
the beavers have shut down a local stream
flooding his one cash crop, neat rows of pines
he'd planned to harvest for Christmases to come.
Their tips are beanpoles now, sticking up through ice.
We skate on the newborn pond, we thump on the roof
of the lodge and squat there, listening for life.

Trouble with this country is, there's more
beavers than people in it. Henry gums
milk toast experimentally, still sore
from the painless dentist who emptied out his mouth.
Trouble is, these Conservation bums
—they're only kids, y'know, with blasting caps—
they'd rather blow the dam up than set traps,
traps is work. *By damn! They'll drive me out.*

Measurers live here, rat-shaped and tough,
with cutting tools for teeth and tails that serve
as plasterers' trowels. Where aspen's not enough
they go to birch and apple rather than starve.
Whatever tree they fell they cut the wood
in thirty-six-inch lengths. They're rarely off
that mark more than an inch or two. And what
they don't build with they store for winter food.

Henry hears their nightwork from his bed.
His phantom teeth are killing him again.
Traps! You got to trap the kit inside!
Layer by layer the lodge is packed with mud
and board by batten his view of things falls in.

Birthday Poem

I am born at home
the last of four children.
The doctor brings me as promised
in his snap-jawed black leather satchel.

He takes me out in sections
fastens limbs to torso
torso to neck stem
pries Mama's navel open
and inserts me, head first.

Chin back, I swim upward
up the alimentary canal
bypassing mouth and nose holes
and knock at the top
of her head to be let out
wherefore her little bald spot.

Today my mother is eighty-two
splendidly braceleted and wigged.
She had to go four times to the well
to get me.

Changing the Children

Anger does this.
Wishing the furious wish
turns the son into a crow
the daughter, a porcupine.

Soon enough, no matter how
we want them to be happy
our little loved ones, no
matter how we prod them
into our sun that it may
shine on them, they whine
to stand in the dry-goods store.
Fury slams in.
The willful fury befalls.

Now the varnish-black son in a tree
crow the berater, denounces the race
of fathers, and the golden daughter
all arched bristle and quill
leaves scribbles on the tree bark
writing how The Nameless One
accosted her in the dark.

How put an end to this cruel spell?
Drop the son from the tree with a rifle.
Introduce maggots under his feathers
to eat down to the pure bone of boy.

In spring when the porcupine comes
all stealth and waddle to feed on the willows
stun her with one blow of the sledge
and the entrapped girl will fly out
crying Daddy! or Danny!
or is it Darling?

and we will live all in bliss
for a year and a day until
the legitimate rage of parents
speeds the lad off this time
in the uniform of a toad
who spews a contagion of warts
while the girl contracts to a spider
forced to spin from her midseam
the saliva of false repentance.

Eventually we get them back.
Now they are grown up.
They are much like ourselves.
They wake mornings beyond cure,
not a virgin among them.
We are civil to one another.
We stand in the kitchen
slicing bread, drying spoons,
and tuning in to the weather.

Seeing the Bones

This year again the bruise-colored oak
hangs on eating my heart out
with its slow change, the leaves at last
spiraling end over end like your
letters home that fall Fridays
in the box at the foot of the hill
saying the old news, keeping it neutral.
You ask about the dog, fourteen years
your hero, deaf now as a turnip,
thin as kindling.

In junior high your biology class
boiled a chicken down into its bones
four days at a simmer in my pot,
then wired joint by joint
the re-created hen
in an anatomy project
you stayed home from, sick.

Thus am I afflicted, seeing the bones.
How many seasons walking
on fallen apples like pebbles in
the shoes of the Canterbury faithful
have I kept the garden up
with leaven of wood ash, kitchen leavings
and the sure reciprocation of horse dung?

How many seasons have the foals
come right or breeched or in good time

turned yearlings, two-year-olds, and at three
clattered off in a ferment to the sales?
Your ponies, those dapple-gray kings
of the orchard, long gone to skeleton,
gallop across the landscape of my dreams.
I meet my father there, dead years before
you left us for a European career.
He is looping the loop on a roller coaster
called Mercy, he is calling his children in.

I do the same things day by day.
They steady me against the wrong turn,
the closed-ward babel of anomie.
This Friday your letter in thinnest blue
script alarms me. Weekly you grow
more British with your *I shalls*
and now you're off to Africa
or Everest, daughter of the file drawer,
citizen of no return. I give
your britches, long outgrown, to the crows,
your boots with a summer visit's worth
of mud caked on them to the shrews
for nests if they will have them.

Working backward I reconstruct
you. Send me your baby teeth, some new
nail parings and a hank of hair
and let me do the rest. I'll
set the pot to boil.

Sunbathing on a Rooftop in Berkeley

Eleven palm trees stand up between me
and the Bay. A quarter turn and I'm
in line with Campanile Tower.
The hippies are sunbathing too.
They spread themselves out on the sidewalks
with their ingenious crafts for sale
and their humble puppies. We are
all pretending summer is eternal.
Mount Tamalpais hovers in the distance.

I pinch myself: that this is California!
But behind my lightstruck eyelids I am also
a child again in an amusement park
in Pennsylvania, and forty years blow
in and out adapting, as the fog does,
to conditions in the Bay.

My daughter has gone to her class in Criminal
Procedure. She pulls her hair back in a twist.
Maybe she will marry the young man she lives with?
I take note how severely
she regards the laws of search and seizure.
She moves with the assurance of a cheetah.
Still, marriage may be the sort of entrapment
she wishes to avoid? She is all uncertainties,
as I am in this mothering business.

O summers without end, the exact truth is
we are expanding sideways as haplessly

as in the mirrors of the Fun House.
We bulge toward the separate fates that await us
sometimes touching, as sleeves will, whether
or not a hug was intended.

O summers without end, the truth is
no matter how I love her, Death
blew up my dress that day
while she was in the egg unconsidered.

The Envelope

It is true, Martin Heidegger, as you have written,
I fear to cease, even knowing that at the hour
of my death my daughters will absorb me, even
knowing they will carry me about forever
inside them, an arrested fetus, even as I carry
the ghost of my mother under my navel, a nervy
little androgynous person, a miracle
folded in lotus position.

Like those old pear-shaped Russian dolls that open
at the middle to reveal another and another, down
to the pea-sized, irreducible minim,
may we carry our mothers forth in our bellies.
May we, borne onward by our daughters, ride
in the Envelope of Almost-Infinity,
that chain letter good for the next twenty-five
thousand days of their lives.

Body and Soul:
A Meditation

Mornings, after leg lifts and knee bends,
I go up in a shoulder stand.
It's a form of redress. My
winter melancholy hangs
upside down. All my organs
reverse their magnetic fields:
ovaries bob on their eyestalks,
liver, kidneys, spleen, whatever
is in there functioning unseen,
free-float like parachutes,
or so it seems from Plough position,
legs behind my head, two
big toenails grazing the floor.

Body, Old Paint, Old Partner,
I ought to have paid closer
attention when Miss Bloomberg
shepherded the entire fifth grade
into the Walk-Through Woman.
I remember going
up three steps, all right,
to enter the left auricle.
I remember the violet light
which made it churchly
and the heartbeat amplified
to echo from chamber to chamber
like God speaking unto Moses.

But there was nothing about the soul,
that miners' canary flitting
around the open spaces;
no diagram in which
the little ball-bearing soul
bumbled her way downhill
in the pinball machine
of the interior, clicking
against the sternum,
the rib cage, the pelvis.
The Walk-Through Woman ceased
shortly below the waist.
Her genitals were off limits.

Perhaps there the soul
had set up housekeeping?
Perhaps a Pullman kitchen,
a one-room studio
in an erogenous zone?
O easy erogenous zones!
Flashing lights, detour
and danger signs in
the sprouting pubic hair.
Alas, I emerged from
the right ventricle
little the wiser.

Still unlocated, drifting,
my airmail half-ounce soul
shows up from time to time
like those old-fashioned
doctors who used to cheer

their patients in girls' boarding schools
with midnight bedside visits.

Body, Old Paint, Old Partner
in this sedate roundup we ride,
going up the Mountain in
the meander of our middle age
after the same old cracked tablets,
though soul and we touch tongue,

somehow it seems less sure;
somehow it seems we've come
too far to get us there.

How It Is

Shall I say how it is in your clothes?
A month after your death I wear your blue jacket.
The dog at the center of my life recognizes
you've come to visit, he's ecstatic.
In the left pocket, a hole.
In the right, a parking ticket
delivered up last August on Bay State Road.
In my heart, a scatter like milkweed,
a flinging from the pods of the soul.
My skin presses your old outline.
It is hot and dry inside.

I think of the last day of your life,
old friend, how I would unwind it, paste
it together in a different collage,
back from the death car idling in the garage,
back up the stairs, your praying hands unlaced,
reassembling the bits of bread and tuna fish
into a ceremony of sandwich,
running the home movie backward to a space
we could be easy in, a kitchen place
with vodka and ice, our words like living meat.

Dear friend, you have excited crowds
with your example. They swell
like wine bags, straining at your seams.
I will be years gathering up our words,
fishing out letters, snapshots, stains,
leaning my ribs against this durable cloth
to put on the dumb blue blazer of your death.

Splitting Wood at Six Above

I open a tree.
In the stupefying cold
—ice on bare flesh a scald—
I seat the metal wedge
with a few left-handed swipes,
then with a change of grips
lean into the eight-pound sledge.

It's muslin overhead.
Snow falls as heavy as salt.
You are four months dead.
The beech log comes apart
like a chocolate nougat.
The wood speaks
first in the tiny voice
of a bird cry, a puppet-squeak,
and then all in a rush,
all in a passionate stammer.
The papery soul of the beech
released by wedge and hammer
flies back into air.

Time will do this as fair
to hickory, birch, black oak,
easing the insects in
till rot and freeze combine
to raise out of wormwood cracks,
blue and dainty, the souls.

They are thin as an eyelash.
They flap once, going up.

The air rings like a bell.
I breathe out drops—
cold morning ghost-puffs
like your old cigarette cough.
See you tomorrow, you said.
You lied.
We're far from finished! I'm still
talking to you (last night's dream);
we'll split the phone bill.
It's expensive calling
from the other side.

Even waking it seems
logical—
your small round
stubbornly airborne soul,
that sun-yellow daisy heart
slipping the noose of its pod,
scooting over the tightrope,
none the worse for its trip,
to arrive at the other side.

It is the sound
of your going I drive
into heartwood. I stack
my quartered cuts bark down,
open yellow-face up.

Late Snow

It's frail, this spring snow, it's pot cheese
packing down underfoot. It flies out of the trees
at sunrise like a flock of migrant birds.
It slips in clumps off the barn roof,
wingless angels dropped by parachute.
Inside, I hear the horses knocking
aimlessly in their warm brown lockup,
testing the four known sides of the box
as the soul must, confined under the breastbone.
Horses blowing their noses, coming awake,
shaking the sawdust bedding out of their coats.
They do not know what has fallen
out of the sky, colder than apple bloom,
since last night's hay and oats.
They do not know how satisfactory
they look, set loose in the April sun,
nor what handsprings are turned under
my ribs with winter gone.

The Excrement Poem

It is done by us all, as God disposes, from
the least cast of worm to what must have been
in the case of the brontosaur, say, spoor
of considerable heft, something awesome.

We eat, we evacuate, survivors that we are.
I think these things each morning with shovel
and rake, drawing the risen brown buns
toward me, fresh from the horse oven, as it were,

or culling the alfalfa-green ones, expelled
in a state of ooze, through the sawdust bed
to take a serviceable form, as putty does,
so as to lift out entire from the stall.

And wheeling to it, storming up the slope,
I think of the angle of repose the manure
pile assumes, how sparrows come to pick
the redelivered grain, how inky-cap

coprinus mushrooms spring up in a downpour.
I think of what drops from us and must then
be moved to make way for the next and next.
However much we stain the world, spatter

it with our leavings, make stenches, defile
the great formal oceans with what leaks down,
trundling off today's last barrowful,
I honor shit for saying: We go on.

In April, in Princeton

They are moving the trees in Princeton.
Full-grown and burlapped, aboard two-ton
trucks, great larches go up the main artery
—once the retreat route of Washington's army—
to holes in the ground I know nothing of.
They are moving the trees for money and love.

They are changing the grass in Princeton
as well. They are bringing it in from sod farms
rolled tight as a church-wedding carpet, unrolled
on the lawn's raw skin in place of the old
onion grass, acid moss, dandelions.
The eye rests, approving. Order obtains.

There is no cure for beauty so replete
it hurts in Princeton. In April, here's such light
and such benevolence that winter
is overlooked, like bad table manners.
Peach, pear, and cherry bloom. The mockingbirds
seize the day, a bunch of happy drunkards

and mindful it will pass, I hurry each noon
to yoga in the Hillel Reading Room
where Yahweh and Krishna intersect in Princeton;
where, under my navel in lotus position
by sending fresh *prana* to the center
albeit lunchless, the soul may enter.

Here, let me not forget Antonin Artaud
who feared to squat, lest his immortal soul
fly out of his anus and disappear
from the madhouse in thin air.
Let me remember how I read these words
in my square white office, its windows barred

by sunlight through dust motes, my own asylum
for thoughts unsorted as to phylum.
Cerulean-blue rug softening the floor,
desk, chair, books, nothing more
except for souls aloft—Artaud's, perhaps,
and mine—drifting like the waxy cups

of white magnolias that drop their porcelain
but do not shatter, in April, in Princeton.

July, Against Hunger

All week the rain holds off. We sweat
stuffing the barn full, like a pillow,
as much as it will hold of these
strangely dead, yellow cubes we set
in unchinked rows, so air can move between.
The smell collects, elusive, sweet,
of gray nights flecked with the snake tongue
of heat lightning, when the grownups sat
late on the side porch talking politics,
foreclosures, war, and Roosevelt.

Loneliness fills me like a pitcher.
The old deaths dribble out. My father clucks
his tongue, disapproving of manual labor.
I swivel to catch his eye, he ducks
behind the tractor, his gray fedora
melts into this year's colt munching grain.
Meanwhile, a new life kicks in the mare.
Meanwhile, the poised sky opens on rain.
The time on either side of *now* stands fast
glinting like jagged window glass.

There are limits, my God, to what I can heft
in this heat! Clearly, the Great Rat waits,
who comes all winter to gnaw on iron
or wood, and tears the last flesh from the bone.

The Survival Poem

I saw a picture of a market stall in the morning paper and under the picture was written, "The dreaded rutabaga has again made its appearance . . ." When people talk to me about the Occupation of Paris they mention the dreaded rutabaga.

—*Mavis Gallant,* A Fairly Good Time

Welcome, old swede,
old baggy root,
old bindrag as well
of Bonaparte's troops.
When the horses' nostrils
are webbed with ice
and out of the hay
fall torpid mice
and calves go stiff
in their mothers' wombs
and the apple core
cloaks the tunnel worm;
when the soldiers' bandages
hung out to dry
clatter like boards
in the four o'clock sky
and the last blood runs
from the bulbs of the beets
and the cabbages shed
their hundred sheets,
welcome, old swede,
strong-smelling Bigfoot.
In the camps all ate
from the same rank pot.

Let me dine with praise
on you alone.
Pray the Lord lay me down
one more time like a stone;
one winter more
from my musty bed
pray the Lord raise me up
in the morn like bread.

Territory

Mistaking him for a leaf, I cut a toad
in two with the power mower and he goes on
lopsidedly hopping until his motor runs out.

By the next pass there is no sign of my carnage.
Now I have cut a swath around the perimeter
declaring this far the grass is tamed.

I think of the wolf who marks his territory
with urine, and where there is wolf there is
the scientist who follows him, yellowing

the same pines at the same intervals
until the baffled creature, worn out
with producing urea, cedes his five acres.

We are not of it, but in it. We are
in it willynilly with our machinery
and measurements, and all for the good.

One rarely sees the blood of the toad.

How It Goes On

Today I trade my last unwise
ewe lamb, the one who won't leave home,
for two cords of stove-length oak
and wait on the old enclosed
front porch to make the swap.
November sun revives the thick
trapped buzz of horseflies. The siren
for noon and forest fires blows
a sliding scale. The lamb of woe
looks in at me through glass
on the last day of her life.

Geranium scraps from the window box
trail from her mouth, burdock burrs
are stickered to her fleece like chicken pox,
under her tail stub, permanent smears.

I think of how it goes on,
this dark particular bent of our hungers:
the way wire eats into a tree
year after year on the pasture's perimeter,
keeping the milk cows penned
until they grow too old to freshen;
of how the last wild horses were scoured
from canyons in Idaho, roped, thrown,
their nostrils twisted shut with wire
to keep them down, the mares aborting
days later, all of them carted to town.

I think of how it will be
in January, nights so cold
the pond ice cracks like target practice,
daylight glue-colored, sleet falling,
my yellow horse slick with the ball-bearing
sleet, raising up from his dingy browse
out of boredom and habit
to strip bark from the fenced-in trees;
of February, month of the hard palate,
the split wood running out,
worms working in the flour bin.

The lamb, whose time has come, goes off
in the cab of the dump truck, tied to the seat
with baling twine, durable enough
to bear her to the knife and rafter.

O lambs! The whole wolf-world sits down to eat
and cleans its muzzle after.

from

Our Ground Time Here Will Be Brief

Our Ground Time Here Will Be Brief

Blue landing lights make
nail holes in the dark.
A fine snow falls. We sit
on the tarmac taking on
the mail, quick freight,
trays of laboratory mice,
coffee and Danish for
the passengers.

Wherever we're going
is Monday morning.
Wherever we're coming from
is Mother's lap.
On the cloud-pack above, strewn
as loosely as parsnip
or celery seeds, lie
the souls of the unborn:

my children's children's
children and their father.
We gather speed for the last run
and lift off into the weather.

Rejoicing with Henry

Not that he holds with church, but Henry goes
Christmas morning in a tantrum of snow,
Henry, who's eighty-two and has no kin
and doesn't feature prayer, but likes the singing.

By afternoon the sun is visible,
a dull gun-metal glint. We come to call
bearing a quart of home-made wine a mile
and leading Babe, our orphaned hand-raised foal.

This gladdens Henry, who stumps out to see
Babe battle the wooden bridge. Will she
or won't she? Vexed with a stick she leaps across
and I'm airborne as well. An upstate chorus
on Henry's radio renders loud
successive verses of "Joy to the World."

In spite of all the balsam growing free
Henry prefers a store-bought silver tree.
It's lasted him for years, the same
crimped angel stuck on top. Under, the same
square box from the Elks. Most likely shaving cream,
says Henry, who seldom shaves or plays the host.

Benevolent, he pours the wine. We toast
the holiday, the filly beating time
in his goat shed with her restive hooves. That's youth,
says Henry when we go to set her loose,

Never mind. Next year, if I live that long,
she'll stand in the shafts. Come Christmas Day
we'll drive that filly straight to town.
Worth waiting for, that filly. Nobody says

the word aloud: *Rejoice.* We plod
home tipsily and all uphill to boot,
the pale day fading as we go
leaving our odd imprints in the snow
to mark a little while the road
ahead of night's oncoming thick clubfoot.

Henry Manley Looks Back

Snapping kindling for the kitchen stove
Henry breaks his hip. Once he's pinned
and feeling wintry, neighbors take him in,
take in his daddy's chair, his reading lamp
—gooseneck, circa 1910—take Scamp,
his skinny whippet, in as well. Henry loves
his new life as the sage of yesteryear,
its mythic blizzards, droughts and forest fires
when he yoked oxen, killed bears, swilled applejack
and in dense snow fog brought the milk cows back
by single lantern. Meanwhile, porcupines
have entered Henry's house and set up camp.
Part of the caved-in roof now forms a ramp
for other creatures who've trooped in to raise
their young. Henry, having crutched there, says
You can't look back, and stands, bracing his spine
against the door jamb of his lost kingdom.
Scamp pokes her narrow muzzle in his palm.
The spring thaw starts, orderly and calm.

Feeding Time

Sunset. I pull on
parka, boots, mittens, hat,
cross the road to the paddock.
Cat comes,
the skinny, feral tom
who took us on last fall.
Horses are waiting.
Each enters his box
in the order they've all
agreed on, behind my back.
Cat supervises from the molding cove.
Hay first. Water next. Grain last.
Check thermometer: seven degrees.
Check latches. Leave.

The sky
goes purple, blotched with red.
Feed dog next.
I recross the road to the woodshed.
Snappish moment with cat
but no real contest.
Wag, wag, kerchunk! The plate
is polished. Dog
grovels his desire
to go inside, lie like a log
by the fire.

Two above.
Above, it's gray

with meager afterglow.
Feed birds next.
I wade by way
of footprint wells through deep snow
to cylinders on trees.
Cat follows
observing distribution
of sunflower seeds.
Checks out each heel-toe
I've stepped in, in case
something he needs,
something small and foolish lurks.
No luck.

Penultimate,
cat gets
enormous supper:
chicken gizzards! Attacks
these like a cougar
tearing, but not in haste.
Retires to barn loft
to sleep in the hay,
or pretends to. Maybe
he catches dessert this way.

Now us,
Dear One. My soup, your bread
in old blue bowls that have withstood
thirty years of slicings and soppings.
Where are the children
who ate their way through helpings
of cereals and stews
to designs of horse, pig,

sheep on view
at the bottom of the dish?
Crying, *when I grow up*,
children have got their wish.

It's ten below.
The house dozes.
The attic stringers cough.
Time that blows on the kettle's rim
waits to carry us off.

In the Pea Patch

These as they clack in the wind
saying castanets, saying dance with me,
saying do me, dangle their intricate
nuggety scrota

and these with the light shining through
call up a woman in a gauzy dress
young, with tendrils of hair at her neck,
leaning in a summer doorway

and as the bloom of the lime-green pod
rubs away under the polishing thumb
in the interior
sweet for the taking, nine little fetuses
nod their cloned heads.

Relearning the Language of April

Where this man walks his fences
the willows do pliés with green laces,
eyelashes fly from the white plums,
the gaunt elms begin to open their frames.

When he passes, lithe with morning,
the terriers, rump-deep in a chuckhole,
boom out to follow,
the squirrels chirrup like cardinals.

Five prick-eared ponies
lift from their serious chewing.
The doomed cattle, wearing
intelligent smiles, turn.

For miles around, the plowed fields
release a sweet rancidness
warm as sperm.

I lie in the fat lap of noon
overhearing the doves' complaint.
Far off, a stutter of geese raise alarms.

Once more, Body, Old Paint,
how could you trick me like this
in spring's blowzy arms?

Continuum: a Love Poem

going for grapes with
ladder and pail in
the first slashing rain
of September rain
steeping the dust
in a joyous squelch the sky
standing up like steam
from a kettle of grapes
at the boil wild fox grapes
wickedly high tangled in must
of cobweb and bug spit
going for grapes year
after year we two with
ladder and pail stained
with the rain of grapes
our private language

Family Reunion

The week in August you come home,
adult, professional, aloof,
we roast and carve the fatted calf
—in our case home-grown pig, the chine
garlicked and crisped, the applesauce
hand-pressed. Hand-pressed the greengage wine.

Nothing is cost-effective here.
The peas, the beets, the lettuces
hand sown, are raised to stand apart.
The electric fence ticks like the slow heart
of something we fed and bedded for a year,
then killed with kindness's one bullet
and paid Jake Mott to do the butchering.

In winter we lure the birds with suet,
thaw lungs and kidneys for the cat.
Darlings, it's all a circle from the ring
of wire that keeps the raccoons from the corn
to the gouged pine table that we lounge around,
distressed before any of you was born.

Benign and dozy from our gluttonies,
the candles down to stubs, defenses down,
love leaking out unguarded the way
juice dribbles from the fence when grounded
by grass stalks or a forgotten hoe,
how eloquent, how beautiful you seem!

Wearing our gestures, how wise you grow,
ballooning to overfill our space,
the almost parents of your parents now.
So briefly having you back to measure us
is harder than having let you go.

Leaving My Daughter's House

I wake to the sound of horses' hooves clacking
on cobblestones, a raucous, irregular rhythm.
Mornings, the exercise boys, young Algerians
from the stable next door, take their assigned
animals into the Forêt de Soignes for a gallop.

In Belgium all such menial work is done
by Arabs or Turks. Barefoot, shivering
in the north light of 8 a.m. I stand
twitching the curtain aside to admire
the casual crouch of small men in the saddle,
their birdlike twitters, their debonair
cigarettes, and the crush of excitable horses
milling about, already lather-flecked.

I know that these skinny colts are second-rate runners.
They'll never turn up in silks at Ascot or Devon.
The closest they'll get to the ocean
is to muddy the oval track at Ostende
for the summer vacation crowd braving the drizzle
to snack on waffles or pickled eel between races.

And no matter how hard I run I know
I can't penetrate my daughter's life
in this tiny Flemish town where vectors of glass
roofs run to the horizon. Tomatoes climb
among grapes in all the greenhouses of Hoeilaart.
Although it is March, the immense purple faces

of last summer's cabbages, as if choleric
from the work of growing, still loll in the garden.

At odd hours in the rain (it is nearly
always raining) I hear the neighbor's rooster
clear-calling across the patchwork farm
where I walk among sheep the height and heft
of ponies. Their gravelly *baas* rumble
an octave lower than their American cousins.

What a Crusoe place this is, juicily rained on,
emerald-thick! What a bide-a-wee I visit
playing a walk-on part with my excursion ticket
that does not prevent my caring with secret frenzy
about this woman, this child no longer a child.

The horses are coming back now, making a calmer
metrical clatter in four-four time. Tomorrow
when they set out again, arching their swans' necks,
I will have crossed the ocean, gone beyond time
where we stand in a mannerly pose at the window
watching the ancient iron strike flint from stones,
balancing on the bit that links us and keeps us
from weeping O God! into each other's arms.

February

First waking to the gray
of linsey-woolsey cloth
the vivid spotted dogs
the red-fox cattle and
the meeker-colored horses
flattened in snow fog

first waking into gray
flecked with common cock-
crow unfolding the same
chilblain-bruised feet
the old shoulder ache
Mama every day

remembering how you won
the death you wished for
the death you sidled up to
remembering how

like a child in late afternoon
drained from the jubilant sledding
you were content to coast
the run-out to a stop

booted and capped in the barn
joy enters where I haul
a hay bale by its binding string
and with my free hand pull
your easy death along.

Itinerary of an Obsession

Just remember that everything east of you has already happened.

—Advice on a time-zone chart

I ascend over Paris with a planeload of pilgrims,
none under seventy, all clutching
their illustrated texts of the Holy Land
in which clouds shaped like sheep float
through the Patriarch's sky. Next to me
a little leathery woman takes out her teeth
and mines their crevices with a handkerchief.
Two nuns across the way wrap up
the dear little salt and pepper as mementos.
Pas loin, one tells me, fingering her rosary
and pointing up, when
lulled by motion or distance here you come
leaping out of the coffin again,
flapping around the funeral home
crying Surprise! I was only fooling!
while your lovesick dog chases a car
the twin of yours and lies dead
years back in a clump of goldenrod.

Later, in Rome, in St. Peter's Square
when the Pope comes to the window
leaning out over his faded prayer rug
to bless the multitude, cannons are fired.
Many fall to their knees.
I have seen this before, in the rotogravure,
but not how weary the Holy Father looks
nor how frail he is, crackling into the microphone.
I am eating an orange in the static shower

of Latin when, as coolly as Pascal,
you turn up arranging to receive
extreme unction from an obliging priest
with a bad cold. You swivel your head
to keep from inhaling his germs. Pigeons
swoop past, altering the light.
I put my hands in your death
as into the carcass of a stripped turkey.

Next, on the lip of the Red Sea
in a settlement as raw as any frontier town
I meet a man from Omaha who has been detained
for nine hours at the border. They tore
the linings out of his suitcases,
they shredded his toilet kit. Tell me, he asks
from under his immense melancholy mustache,
Do I look like a terrorist? We set
out for Solomon's mines together.
In the ancient desert I stumble through mirages.
The rough red hills arouse armies of slaves,
men wasting away digging and lifting,
dying of thirst in their loincloths.
My feet weep blisters, sand enters the sores,
I bite on sand. On the floor of your closet
smolder a jumble of shoes, stiletto heels,
fleece-lined slippers, your favorite sneakers
gritty from Cape Cod, all my size.

Years pass, as they say in storybooks.
It is true that I dream of you less.
Still, when the phone rings in my sleep
and I answer, a dream-cigarette in my hand,
it is always the same. We are back at our posts,

hanging around like boxers in
our old flannel bathrobes. You haven't changed.
I, on the other hand, am forced to grow older.
Now I am almost your mother's age.
Imagine it! Did you think you could escape?
Eventually I'll arrive in her
abhorrent marabou negligee
trailing her scarves like broken promises
crying yoo-hoo! Anybody home?

Apostrophe to a Dead Friend

on being interviewed by her biographer

Little by little my gender drifts away
leaving the bones of this person
whose shoe size was your size
who traded dresses in our pool
of public-occasion costumes:
yours the formal-length jersey
mine the cocktail wool
and your dead mother's mink coat that
I always said looked like muskrat.

It fades, the glint of those afternoons
we lay in the sun by the pond.
Paler, the intimate confidences.
Even the distances we leapt in poems
have shrunk. No more parapets.
The men have grown smaller, drier,
easier to refuse.
Passion subsides like a sunset.
Urgency has been wrung from the rendezvous.

Now that the children have changed
into exacting adults, the warmth
we felt for each other's young
takes on the skin tone of plain daylight.
However well-fed and rosy
they are no kinder or wiser than we.

Soon I will be sixty.
How it was with you now

hardly more vivid than how
it is without you, I carry
the sheer weight of the telling
like a large infant, on one hip.
I who am remaindered in the conspiracy
doom, doom on my lips.

In Memoriam P.W. Jr.
1921–1980

THE UNFINISHED STORY

A habit I can't break, caring.
In sleep the signs come on long as a freight train.
Long as the college racing shell
he used to flip up, like an umbrella,
this brother I love, in real life shriveled
by a disease that wastes the large muscles.

Tonight he strides in rosy-cheeked
and eighteen in the pectorals
to announce he has six months to live and plans
for every hour: Pompeii, galloping
the moors at Devon, The Great Wall,
lots more sex. Further, he means to kill
time with a perpetual-motion cell.

Stickered like a housefly to the ceiling
a small watcher whispers, *this is*
only a dream. I take it, I run it through.
It is less terrible
than what I wake to.

THE INCEST DREAM

Brother, the story's still unfinished; you
struggle up as best you can,
three-legged now as in the riddle of the Sphinx,

the whole left side of you dumb
to the brain's fiercest commands.
Talking is problematical; vowels distort
rising against the numbness in your throat.

Still, we've been out to dinner,
assorted husbands, wives,
and driving back through rain the sidewise swipe
of memory delivers a lightstruck
picture of us, ages four and six
propped in matching sailor suits
against a railing on the Boardwalk,
both wearing the family lower lip,
the family shock of hair,
two savages spruced up for Grandma's Sunday
in the roller chair.

Listen! I love you!
I've always loved you!
And so we totter and embrace
surrounded in an all-night garage
by theatergoers barking for their cars,
the obedient machines spiraling down
level by level as we block
the exit saying our good-byes,
you tangled in your cane, my black
umbrella flapping like a torn bat.

At 3 a.m. I'm driven to such extremes
that when the sorrowing hangman
brings me your severed penis still
tumescent from the scaffold

yet dried and pressed as faithfully
as a wildflower
I put it away on my closet shelf
and lie back down in my lucky shame.

OUT-OF-THE-BODY TRAVEL

Even close to the end
when nothing works except one hand
my brother goes to the Special Cases pool
where cheerful athletes reposition
his puppet bones in a canvas sling
scoot him down the ramp
into tepid water
adjust his flotation collar
and cut him loose.

Speech has left him, but not joy.
I carry that grin
that broad important self-pleasured wink
with me into the April day.

RETROSPECT IN THE KITCHEN

After the funeral I pick
forty pounds of plums from your tree
Earth Wizard, Limb Lopper
and carry them by DC 10
three thousand miles to my kitchen

and stand at midnight—nine o'clock
your time—on the fourth day of your death

putting some raveled things
unsaid between us into the boiling pot
of cloves, cinnamon, sugar.

Love's royal color
the burst purple fruit bob up.

THE MAN OF MANY L'S

My whole childhood I feared cripples
and how they got that way: the one-
legged Lavender Man who sold
his sachets by St. Mary's steeple,
the blind who tapped past humming what they knew,
even the hunchback seamstress, a ragdoll
who further sagged to pin my mother's hems,
had once been sturdy, had once been whole.
Something entered people, something chopped,
pressed, punctured, had its way with them
and if you looked, bad child, it entered you.

When we found out what the disease would do,
lying, like any council's stalwarts,
all of us swore to play our parts
in the final act at your command.

The first was easy. You gave up your left hand
and the right grew wiser, a juggler for its king.
When the poor dumb leg began to falter
you took up an alpenstock for walking
once flourished Sundays by our dead father.
Month by month the battleground grew thinner.
When you could no longer swallow meat

we steamed and mashed your dinner
and bent your straw to chocolate soda treats.

And when you could not talk, still you could write
questions and answers on a magic slate,
then lift the page, like laundry to the wind.
I plucked the memory splinter from your spine
as we played at being normal, who
had eased each other in the cold zoo
of childhood. Three months before
you died I wheeled you through the streets
of placid Palo Alto to catch
spring in its flamboyant tracks.
You wrote the name of every idiot flower
I did not know. Yucca rained.
Mimosa shone. The bottlebrush took fire
as you fought to hold your great head on its stem.
Lillac, you wrote, *Magnollia. Lilly.*
And further, *olleander. Dellphinium.*

O man of many L's, brother, my wily
resident ghost, may I never spell
these crowfoot dogbane words again
these showy florid words again
except I name them under your spell.

from

The Long Approach

You Are in Bear Country

Advice from a pamphlet published by the
Canadian Minister of the Environment

They've
been here
for thousands of years.
You're
the visitor.
Avoid
encounters. Think ahead.
Keep clear
of berry patches
garbage dumps, carcasses.
On woods walks bring
noisemakers, bells.
Clap hands along the trail
or sing
but in dense bush
or by running water
bear may not hear your clatter.
Whatever else
don't whistle. Whistling
is thought by some to imitate
the sounds bears make when they mate.

You need to know
there are two kinds:
ursus arctus horribilis
or grizzly
and *ursus americanus*
the smaller black

said to be
somewhat less likely to attack.
Alas, a small *horribilis*
is difficult to distinguish
from a large *americanus.*

Although
there is no
guaranteed life-saving way
to deal with an aggressive bear
some ploys
have proved more
successful than others.
Running's a poor choice.
Bear can outrun a racehorse.

Once you're face to face
speak softly. Take
off your pack
and set it down
to distract the grizzly.
Meanwhile back
slowly toward a large
sparsely branched tree
but remember
black bears are agile climbers
in which case
a tree may not offer escape.

As a last resort you can
play dead. Drop
to the ground face down.
In this case

wearing your pack
may shield your body from attack.
Courage. Lie still. Sometimes
your bear may veer away.
If not
bears have been known
to inflict only minor injuries
upon the prone.

Is death
by bear to be preferred
to death by bomb? Under
these extenuating circumstances
your mind may make absurd
leaps. *The answer's yes.*
Come on in. Cherish
your wilderness.

Atlantic City 1939

When I was young and returning from
death's door, I served as chaperone,
pale as waxworks, a holiday child,
under the bear laprobe in the back
of my courtesy uncle's Cadillac
careening through a world gone wild.

The Germans pushed into Poland. My
mother sat up front, close pressed
as bees to honey to Uncle Les
and wobbled the stick he shifted by.
I whooped my leftover cough but said
no word, a bear asleep or dead.

Later, in the Boardwalk arcade
when a chirping photographer made
me put my face in the hole with wings,
they snuggled behind him, winked and smiled
as he fussed and clicked the shutter's spring
and there I was corporeal
in the garb of the angel Gabriel,
forever a captive child.

Pink with ardor, not knowing why,
I longed for one of them to die
that slow September by the sea.
He fell on the beach at Normandy.
I never heard her say his name
again without a flush of shame
for my complicity.

The Chain

My mother's insomnia over at last,
at dawn I enter her bureau drawers.
Under the petticoats, bedjackets, corsets,
under the unfinished knitting that crossed
continents with her, an affable animal,
I come on a hatbox of type-O any-hair,
heavy braids that have lain fifty years in this oval.
Between them, my mother's mother's calling card
engraved on brittle ivory vellum:
Mrs. Abraham Simon, Star Route 3, Radford.

Radford, Virginia, three thousand souls.
Here my mother spent her girlhood, not
without complications, playing
the Methodist church organ for weddings,
funerals, and the Sunday choir.
Here her mother, holding a lily-shaped
ear trumpet, stepped down from the surrey
Grandfather drove forty miles to Roanoke
to witness the blowing of the shofar
on Rosh Hashanah and Yom Kippur.

Affirming my past, our past in
a nation losing its memory, turning
its battlegrounds into parking lots,
slicking its regional differences over
with video games, substituting outer
space for history, I mourn
the type-O any-deaths of Mecca,

Athens, Babylon, Rome,
Radford, country towns
of middle-class hopes and tall corn.

Every year a new itinerant
piano teacher. New exercises
in the key of most-flats. 1908,
the first indoor toilet. The first
running hot water. My mother
takes weekly elocution lessons.
The radio, the telephone,
the Model T arrive. One by one
her sisters are sent north to cousins
in search of kindly Jewish husbands.

Surely having lived this long confers
a kind of aristocracy on my mother,
who kept to the end these talismans,
two dry links in the chain of daughters.
In the land of burley tobacco,
of mules in the narrow furrows,
in the land of diphtheria and strangles,
of revival meetings and stillborn angels,
in the land of eleven living siblings
I make my mother a dowager queen.

I give her back the chipped ruby goblets.
I hand over the battered Sheffield tureen
and the child I was, whose once-auburn hair
she scooped up like gems from the beauty-shop floor.

Introducing the Fathers

for Anne Carpenter

Yours lugs shopping bags of sweet corn
via parlor car to enhance the lunches
of his fellow lawyers at the Century Club.
Sundays he sneaks from church to stretch a net
across the Nissequegue River
and catches shad as they swim up to spawn.

Mine locks up the store six nights at seven,
cracks coconuts apart on the brick hearth,
forces lobsters down in the boiling pot.
Sundays he lolls in silk pajamas,
and swaggers out at nightfall to play pinochle.

In our middle age we bring them back, these despots,
mine in shirtsleeves, yours in summer flannels,
whose war cry was: the best of everything!
and place them side by side, inflatable
Macy daddies ready for the big parade.

We open a friendship between them, sweetly posthumous,
and watch them bulge out twirling Malacca canes
into the simple future of straight losses,
still matching net worths, winning big at blackjack,
our golden warriors rising toward the Big Crash.

Appetite

I eat these
wild red raspberries
still warm from the sun
and smelling faintly of jewelweed
in memory of my father

tucking the napkin
under his chin and bending
over an ironstone bowl
of the bright drupelets
awash in cream

my father
with the sigh of a man
who has seen all and been redeemed
said time after time
as he lifted his spoon

men kill for this.

Grandchild

for Yann

All night the *douanier* in his sentry box
at the end of the lane where France begins plays fox
and hounds with little spurts of cars
that sniff to a stop at the barrier
and declare themselves. I stand at the window
watching the ancient boundaries that flow
between my daughter's life and mine dissolve
like taffy pulled until it melts in half
without announcing any point of strain
and I am a young unsure mother again
stiffly clutching the twelve-limbed raw
creature that broke from between my legs, that stew
of bone and membrane loosely sewn up in
a fierce scared flailing other being.

We blink, two strangers in a foreign kitchen.
Now that you've drained your mother dry and will
not sleep, I take you in my arms, brimful
six days old, little feared-for mouse.
Last week when you were still a fish
in the interior, I dreamed you thus:
The *douanier* brought you curled up in his cap
buttoned and suited like him, authority's prop
—a good Victorian child's myth—
and in his other hand a large round cheese
ready to the point of runniness.
At least there, says the dream, no mysteries.

Toward dawn I open my daughter's cupboard on
a choice of calming teas—*infusions*—
verbena, fennel, linden, camomile,
shift you on my shoulder and fill the kettle.
Age has conferred on me a certain grace.
You're a package I can rock and ease
from wakefulness to sleep. This skill comes back
like learning how to swim. Comes warm and quick
as first milk in the breasts. I comfort you.
Body to body my monkey-wit soaks through.

Later, I wind the outside shutters up.
You sleep mouse-mild, topped with camomile.
Daylight slips past the *douane*. I rinse my cup.
My daughter troubles sleep a little while
longer. The just-milked cows across the way
come down their hillside single file
and the dream, the lefthand gift of ripened brie
recurs, smelly, natural, and good
wanting only to be brought true
in your own time: your childhood.

Caring: a Dream

Sepia the first part
the shuffle of the doomed
like an Indian documentary

a sprawl of dead elephants
and then outlined like a Rouault
great-aunt Manya of the monkey

dirt under her fingernails
gray hairs flying out of her bun
and Beppo on her shoulder

comes back to me in primary colors
comes back noiselessly
in her electric car

straddling the center line
camps with hoboes along the Delaware
the shelf of her bosom swaddled in scarves

every wet tramp starved dog
mauled chipmunk Manya saved
deserved deserved

and especially Beppo of the scarred neck
the hapless organ grinder she rapped
on the head with an umbrella

then appeased with twenty dollars
Beppo who ate with her slept with her
combed her hair kissed her on the lips

deserved deserved O Manya
I want to tell you caring is small
susceptible fits in a pocket

nor is it one thing to save animals
and people another
but seamless

you who were no one's mother
come spraddle legged and sure
with monkey and funny car

framed in this dream
by the shuffle of the doomed
to command me to go on.

Shopping in Ferney with Voltaire

Wearing a flowered nightgown
under his frock coat, Voltaire
comes down the avenue of oaks
a basket on his arm. Looks
four ways at his poète-philosophe
likeness in the square
that vélomoteurs dive toward
careening off to either side
and walks into the crowd
of tidy Genevoises who swarm
each Saturday across the line
to stroll along the cobblestones
choosing among a hundred cheeses
sandbagged sausages
dripping Breton artichokes
oysters, olives, almonds, dates.

A little chitchat seems appropriate.
I ask him how he feels.
Fingering the fringy cornucopias
of black chanterelles
(les trompettes de la mort) he quotes
himself: qui veut voir une ombre?
I've read that in the Besterman
biography. Also about
the colic on demand.
Also the fainting fits
to dispatch hangers-on.

We rummage among the burly roots
fresh dug from local plots.
He chooses small white turnips
to tuck around the Sunday roast.
I tell him his remains
were exhumed thirteen years post-mortem.
Someone stole two teeth and his left foot.
He shrugs. —A useless passion,
necrophilia. About
that stupid recantation:
remember that I never took
communion! Let's be clear on that.
I told the Abbé, you will note
I'm spitting blood.
We must be careful not
to mingle mine with God's.
He grins. We stop at carts of citrus fruits
collect a dozen clementines
and pay with clanks of old-style coins.

One booth away
Amnesty International
has prisoners for sale.
Handbills cry aloud
the murdered, the disappeared,
the tortured, in before-
and-after photographs.
A self-improvement course
run riot in reverse.
Anyone who cares to can
adopt a prisoner of conscience.
Voltaire's list is longer than
old-school homework Latin scansions.

In my day—he sighs
reliving the stench of pain
—torture was a public act.
Before they killed a man
they broke him on the rack.
The main thing was to die
courageously. It's different now.
No longer personal.
His sharp fox face so like
Max Adrian's Pangloss
as if he had just caught
out of the corner of his eye
the murderings en masse.
The nuclear juggernaut.
The Great Beast lumbering past.
The labor camps, the stripping off
of civilization's mask.

We walk together toward
the border at Meyrin.
The sky goes yellow as
old corn shucks. Rain will drench
the ancient hills, thorn-fenced,
these stubbled fields, the cows
kneeling along the ridge.
Behind us, Ferney brims with light.
—Adieu, he says. —Take my advice.
Always live close to the edge
so that when sudden flight
is called for, you can put
a foot down on the other side.
We embrace three times, à la Suisse.
I cross the douane, then turn

to watch the old philosopher
mushrooms, roots and tangerines in hand
limp back to the Enlightenment
and disappear.

At a Private Showing in 1982

for Gillian Anderson

This loving attention to the details:
faces by Bosch and Bruegel,
the mélange of torture tools,
the carpentry of the stake,
the Catherine wheel,
the bars, spires, gibbets, pikes—
I confess my heart sank
when they brought out the second reel . . .

Anorectic Jeanne d'Arc,
how long it takes her
to burn to death in this picture!
When monks fast, it is called ascetic.
The film beamed on the dining-room wall
of an old brownstone
undergoing gentrification on Capitol Hill,
glass shards and daffodils
on alternate lawns,
harpsichord, bare board table,
cheese, nuts, jug wine,

and striding across the screen,
hauntingly young, unbowed,
not yet absurd, not yet insane,
Antonin Artaud in a bit part:
the "good" priest,
the one who declaims
"You are persecuting a saint!"

but does not offer
to die beside her.

And how is any of this
different today,
except now in color, and talky—
this prurient close
examination of pain,
fanaticism, terror?

Though the judges dress
like World War I British
soldiers in tin helmets
and Sam Browne belts,
though the music exactly
matches the mouthed words,
though Jeanne's
enormous wounded-doe's eyes
roll up or shut down
in hope, in anguish,
though Renée Falconetti,
who plays this part, was merely
a comic-stage actress
and never shows up on celluloid again,
though Artaud
tonsured for the set
walks the streets of Paris
in costume in 1928
and is mocked by urchins
and is peppered with catcalls,
what does it profit us?

Artaud will die in the madhouse
in terror for his immortal soul,
Falconetti will drop out of sight,
an émigrée in the Argentine,
we few will finish the wine
and skulk out on this spring night
together, unsafe on Capitol Hill.

In the Absence of Bliss

Museum of the Diaspora, Tel Aviv

The roasting alive of rabbis
in the ardor of the Crusades
went unremarked in *Europe from*
the Holy Roman Empire to 1918,
open without prerequisite
when I was an undergraduate.

While reciting the Sh'ma in full
expectation that their souls
would waft up to the bosom
of the Almighty the rabbis burned,
pious past the humming extremes
of pain. And their loved ones with them.
Whole communities tortured and set aflame
in Christ's name
while chanting Hear, O Israel.

Why?
Why couldn't the rabbis recant,
kiss the Cross, pretend?
Is God so simple that He can't
sort out real from sham?
Did He want
these fanatic autos-da-fé, admire
the eyeballs popping,
the corpses shrinking in the fire?

We live in an orderly
universe of discoverable laws,

writes an intelligent alumna
in *Harvard Magazine.*
Bliss is belief,
agnostics always say
a little condescendingly
as befits mandarins who function
on a higher moral plane.

Consider our contemporary
Muslim kamikazes
hurling their explosives-
packed trucks through barriers.
Isn't it all the same?
They too die cherishing the fond
certitude of a better life beyond.

We walk away from twenty-two
graphic centuries of kill-the-jew
and hail, of all things, a Mercedes
taxi. The driver is Yemeni,
loves rock music and hangs
each son's picture—three so far—
on tassels from his rearview mirror.

I do not tell him that in Yemen
Jewish men, like women, were forbidden
to ride their donkeys astride,
having just seen this humiliation
illustrated on the Museum screen.

When his parents came
to the Promised Land, they entered
the belly of an enormous

silver bird, not knowing whether
they would live or die.
No matter. As it was written,
the Messiah had drawn nigh.

I do not ask, who tied
the leaping ram inside the thicket?
Who polished, then blighted the apple?
Who loosed pigs in the Temple,
set tribe against tribe
and nailed man in His pocket?

But ask myself, what would
I die for and reciting what?
Not for Yahweh, Allah, Christ,
those patriarchal fists
in the face. But would
I die to save a child?
Rescue my lover? Would
I run into the fiery barn
to release animals,
singed and panicked, from their stalls?

Bliss is belief, but where's
the higher moral plane I roost on?
This narrow plank given to splinters.
No answers. Only questions.

Video Cuisine

They are weighing the babies again on color television.
They are hanging these small bags of bones up in canvas
  slings
to determine which ones will receive the dried-milk mush,
the concentrate made out of ground-up trash fish.

For years we have watched them, back-lit by the desert,
these miles of dusty hands holding out goatskins or cups,
their animals dead or dying of rinderpest,
and after the credits come up I continue to sit

through *Dinner with Julia*, where, in a French fish
poacher big enough for a small brown baby, an
Alaska salmon simmers in a court bouillon.
For a first course, steak tartare to awaken the palate.

With it Julia suggests a zinfandel. This scene
has a polite, a touristy flavor to it,
and I let it play. But somewhere Oxfam goes on
spooning gluey gruel between the parched lips

of potbellied children, the ones who perhaps can be saved
from kwashiorkor—an ancient Ghanaian word—
though with probable lowered IQs, the voiceover explains,
caused by protein deficiencies linked to the drought

and the drought has grown worse with the gradual increase
  in herds
overgrazing the thin forage grasses of the Sahel.

This, says the voice, can be laid to the natural greed
of the nomad deceived by technicians digging new wells

which means (a slow pan of the sand) that the water table has
  dropped.
And now to Julia's table is borne the resplendent fish.
Always the camera is angled so that the guests look up.
Among them I glimpse that sly Dean, Jonathan Swift.

After the credits come up I continue to sit
with those who are starving to death in a distant nation
squatting, back-lit by the desert, hands out, in my head
and the Dublin Dean squats there too, observing the population

that waits for too little dried milk, white rice, trash fish.
Always the camera is angled so they look up
while their babies are weighed in slings on color television,
look into our living rooms and the shaded rooms we sleep in.

How to Survive Nuclear War

after reading Ibuse's Black Rain

Brought low in Kyoto,
too sick with chills and fever
to take the bullet train to Hiroshima,
I am jolted out of this geography,
pursued by Nazis, kidnapped, stranded
when the dam bursts, my life
always in someone else's hands.
Room service brings me tea and aspirin.

This week the Holy Radish
Festival, pure white daikons
one foot long grace all the city's shrines.
Earlier, a celebration for the souls
of insects farmers may have trampled on
while bringing in the harvest.
Now shall I repent?
I kill to keep whatever
pleases me. Last summer
to save the raspberries
I immolated hundreds of coppery
Japanese beetles.

In some respects,
Ibuse tells me,
radiation sickness is less
terrible than cancer. The hair
comes out in patches. Teeth
break off like matchsticks
at the gum line but the loss

is painless. Burned skin itches,
peels away in strips.
Everywhere the black rain fell
it stains the flesh like a tattoo
but weeks later, when
survivors must expel
day by day in little pisses
the membrane lining the bladder
pain becomes an extreme grammar.

I understand we did this.
I understand
we may do this again
before it is done to us.
In case it is thought of
to do to us.

Just now, the homage that
I could not pay the irradiated dead
gives rise to a dream.
In it, a festival to mourn
the ritual maiming of the ginkgo,
pollarding that lops
all natural growth
from the tumorous stump
years of pruning creates.
I note that these faggots
are burned. I observe that the smoke
is swallowed with great ceremony.
Thereupon every severed shoot
comes back, takes on
a human form, fan-shaped,

ancient, all-knowing,
tattered like us.

This means
we are all to be rescued.

Though we eat animals
and wear their skins,
though we crack mountains
and insert rockets in them

this signifies
we will burn and go up.
We will be burned and come back.

I wake naked, parched,
my skin striped by sunlight.
Under my window
a line of old ginkgos hunkers down.
The new sprouts that break from
their armless shoulders are
the enemies of despair.

Getting Through

I want to apologize
for all the snow falling in
this poem so early in the season.
Falling on the calendar of bad news.
Already we have had snow lucid,
snow surprising, snow bees
and lambswool snow. Already
snows of exaltation have covered
some scars. Larks and the likes
of paisleys went up. But lately the sky
is letting down large-print flakes
of old age. Loving this poor place,
wanting to stay on, we have endured
an elegiac snow of whitest jade,
subdued biographical snows
and public storms, official and profuse.

Even if the world is ending
you can tell it's February
by the architecture of the pastures.
Snow falls on the pregnant mares,
is followed by a thaw, and then
refreezes so that everywhere
their hill upheaves into a glass mountain.
The horses skid, stiff-legged, correct
position, break through the crust
and stand around disconsolate
lipping wisps of hay.

Animals are said to be soulless.
Unable to anticipate.

No mail today.
No newspapers. The phone's dead.
Bombs and grenades, the newly disappeared,
a kidnapped ear, go unrecorded
but the foals flutter inside
warm wet bags that carry them
eleven months in the dark.
It seems they lie transversely, thick
as logs. The outcome is well known.
If there's an April
in the last frail snow of April
they will knock hard to be born.

Out in It

Crouched under my desk, at a bad clap
eighty pounds of spotted dog quakes.
I too lose my head in a storm like this
or would like at least to bury it.
Each time the white knife slashes
the barn cats tunnel deeper into hay.
The horses wheel and gallop while
cymbals clash overhead. They do not know
what trouble they're in wearing
their iron shoes out there in the pasture
when the serpent's tongue darts down
to lick salt from the earth. Last year
one hundred and some-odd people died
in the USA, seized where they stood
under old trees at the edge of the eighteenth tee
or racing out back to snatch bedsheets
off the line.
But these are small shocks,
these pyrotechnics, Hephaestus twiddling his thumbs.
Do not ask me to feel too much here at the fulcrum!

Inside me a whole city
a flagdraped nation
of down vests and L.L. Bean boots
a great big grapefruit
of a planet that is 70% ocean
and 25,000 miles around

is waiting. Where do we want
to be when the first strike comes?
Out in it with all our kith and kin
crisping in one another's arms.

My Elusive Guest

Thoreau loved the grayness of them, homespun
with leafy horns like lichen made of bone.
God's own horses, poor timid creatures, he said
in 1846 in THE MAINE WOODS
and then went on to wonder why they stood
so high at the shoulders, why so long a head,
no tail to speak of. *How like the camelopard,*
he said, rolling the archaic word
on his tongue: *high before and low behind*
and stayed admiring them, upwind.

A hundred years later, the widow Blau
whose rockbound farm I now inhabit
broomed a moose out of her kitchen garden
thinking it the neighbor's brown cow
marauding among the vegetables at dawn
then looked up to behold those rabbit
ears, that wet nearsighted eye
that ferny rack of gray on a still-gray sky
and none since. Spring mornings at first light
sometimes through fog some heavy weight
shifts and wavers against the line of trees
and wanting it in my blood, like a spray
of musk, I beckon the elusive guest,
willing it close. My wild thing, my moose.

Shelling Jacobs Cattle Beans

All summer
they grew unseen
in the corn patch
planted to climb on Silver Queen
Butter and Sugar
compete with witch
grass and lamb's quarters
only to stand naked, old crones,
Mayan, Macedonian
sticks of antiquity
drying alone
after the corn is taken.

I, whose ancestors
put on sackcloth and ashes
for the destruction of the Temple
sit winnowing the beans
on Rosh Hashanah
in the September sun
of New Hampshire.
Each its own example:
a rare bird's egg
cranberry- or blood-flecked
as cool in the hand
as a beach stone
no two exactly alike
yet close as snowflakes.
Each pops out of the dry
husk, the oblong shaft

that held it,
every compartment a tight fit.

I sit on the front stoop
a romantic, thinking
what a centerpiece!
not, what a soup!
layering beans into
their storage jars.
At Pompeii the food
ossified on the table
under strata of ash.
Before that, the Hebrews
stacked bricks
under the Egyptian lash.

Today
in the slums of Lebanon
Semite is set against Semite
with Old Testament fervor.
Bombs go off in Paris,
Damascus, New York,
a network of retaliations.
Where is the God of
my fathers, that I
may pluck Him out of the lineup?
That I may hand back my ticket?

In case we outlast
the winter, in case
when the end comes
ending all matter,

the least gravel
of Jacobs Cattle remain,
let me shell out the lot.
Let me put my faith in the bean.

After the Harvest

Pulling the garden I always think
of starving to death, of how it would be to get by
on what the hard frost left untouched
at the end of the world: a penance of kale,
jerusalem artichokes, brussels sprouts,
some serviceberries, windfall apples
and the dubious bounty of hickory nuts.

Pretty slim pickings for the Tribulation
if that's what this is, preceding
the Rapture I choose to be left out of.
Having never acceded to an initial coming
I hold out no hope for a second
let alone this bland vision of mail-order angels
lifting born-again drivers up from behind the wheel
leaving the rest of us loose on the highways
to play out a rudderless dodgem.

When parents were gods survival was a game
I played in my head, reading by flashlight
under the covers *Swiss Family Robinson*
and *The Adventures of Perrine,* who lived in a hut
and was happy weaving moccasins out of marsh grass.

I longed to be orphaned like her, out on my own,
befriending little creatures of the woods,
never cold or wet or hungry. To be snug

in spite of the world's world is the child-hermit's plan.
Meekly I ate the detested liver and lima beans.

Now all of the gods agree, no part of the main
can survive the nuclear night. And yet,
like a student of mine who is writing a book
on an island linked by once-a-week ferry
to Juneau, where one pay phone and a hot spring bath
suffice for all, in innocent ways we still
need to test the fringe of the freezing dark.
He thinks he can be happy there year round
and the child in me envies his Cave of the Winds.

Meanwhile I fling cornstalks and cucumber,
pea and squash vines across the fence
and the horses mosey over to beg carrot tops.
I am mesmerized by the gesture, handfeeding
feathery greens to the brood mares. This could

be last year or five years or ten years ago
and I sense it is ending, this cycle of saving
and sprouting: a houseful of seedlings in March,
the cutworms of May, June's ubiquitous weeds,
the long August drought peppered with grasshoppers
even as I lop the last purple cabbage, big
as a baby's head, big as my grandson's brain
who on the other side of the world is naming
a surfeit of tropical fruits in five-tone Thai.
A child I long to see again,
growing up in a land where thousands, displaced,
unwanted, diseased, are awash in despair.

Who will put the wafer of survival on their tongues,
lift them out of the camps, restore
their villages, replant their fields, those gardens
that want to bear twelve months of the year?
Who gets Rapture?

Sidelong we catch film clips of the Tribulation
but nobody wants to measure the breadth and length
of the firestorms that lurk in Overkill,
certitude of result through overwhelming strength,
they define it in military circles,

their flyboys swirling up in sunset contrails.
The local kids suit up to bob for apples,
go trick-or-treating on both sides of Main.
November rattles its dry husks down the food chain
on this peaceable island at the top of the hill.

The Long Approach

In the eel-thin belly of the Metro Swearingen
banking in late afternoon over Boston Harbor,
the islands eleven lily pads, my life loose as a frog's,
I try to decipher the meaning of hope rising up again
making music in me all the way from Scranton
where the slag heaps stand like sentries shot dead
at their posts. Hope rising up in my Saab hatchback,
one hundred thousand honest miles on it as I speed
due north from LaBell's cut-rate autopark
to my spiny hillside farm in New Hampshire.

March 21st. Snow still frosts the manure heap
and flurries lace the horses' ample rumps
but in here it's Stephen Foster coming back to me
unexpurgated, guileless, all by heart.
'Tis summer, the darkies are gay, we sang in Miss Dupree's
fifth grade in a suburb that I fled long ago.
Gone are my friends from the cotton fields away
to—an allusion that escaped me—a better land I know.
O the melancholia as I too longed to depart.
Now I belt out Massa's in de cold cold ground
and all the darkies are a'weepin on Route I-93
but what I think of are the French-pastel mornings
daylit at five in my own hills in June when I may
leap up naked, happy, with no more premonition
than the mother of the Pope had. How the same
old pump of joy restarts for me, going home!

What I understand from travel is how luck
hangs in the lefthand lane fifteen miles
over the limit and no cop, no drunk, no ice slick.
Only the lightweight ghosts of racist lyrics
soaring from my throat in common time.
Last week leaving Orlando in a steep climb
my seatmate told me flying horses must be loaded
facing the tail of the plane so they may brace
themselves at takeoff. Otherwise you run
the risk they'll panic, pitch over backward,
smash their hocks. Landing, said the groom,
there is little we can do for them except
pray for calm winds and ask the pilot
to make a long approach.

O brace me, my groom. Pray for calm winds.
Carry me back safely where the snow stands deep in March.
I'm going home the old way with a light hand on the reins
making the long approach.

from

Nurture

Nurture

From a documentary on marsupials I learn
that a pillowcase makes a fine
substitute pouch for an orphaned kangaroo.

I am drawn to such dramas of animal rescue.
They are warm in the throat. I suffer, the critic proclaims,
from an overabundance of maternal genes.

Bring me your fallen fledgling, your bummer lamb,
lead the abused, the starvelings, into my barn.
Advise the hunted deer to leap into my corn.

And had there been a wild child—
filthy and fierce as a ferret, he is called
in one nineteenth-century account—

a wild child to love, it is safe to assume,
given my fireside inked with paw prints,
there would have been room.

Think of the language we two, same and not-same,
might have constructed from sign,
scratch, grimace, grunt, vowel:

Laughter our first noun, and our long verb, howl.

With the Caribou

At the top of the world I want to go for a drive
in a primitive troika lightly harnessed to reindeer.
Behind three clove-brown creatures, yoked together
yet bridleless, guided only by a long pole
that the driver taps to indicate gee and haw
I want to sled over the alpine tundra
race through boreal forests of birch and aspen
and glide past the boggy taiga daggered with black spruce trees.

I want to leap up at the three-nation caribou parley
in Whitehorse, Yukon, to warn them the radionuclides
absorbed from the lichen they live on may kill them
if they don't drown in droves at crossings flooded
out by hydroelectric stations, or slowly
starve to death behind oil pipelines that posit
behavioral barriers they dare not soar over
or burst their aortas trying. I want to advise the species
to set up new herds, to mingle and multiply,

else how can I hurtle with them across the Kobuk River
at Onion Portage, be caught up in the streaming southward,
the harsh crowding of antlers uplifted like thousands
of stump-fingered arms? I'm slithering backward in time to
the Bering land bridge, awash at high tide, I cross over
nibbling down to Nevada, down to New Jersey,
I rejoice to be circumpolar, all of us
on all fours obeying the laws of migration.

In Warm Rooms, Before a Blue Light

All over America tonight,
the males mince past us
gravely tall as dwarves in "Snow White,"

single file, edged with pathos,
a comedy in frock coats played
out on Antarctic ice.

Each bird balances an egg
between his belly and the tops
of his feet, more or less snug

against freezing. Some will drop
as weeks pass and the bizarre parade
exacts its ritual upkeep.

Meanwhile the females swim
far and deep, fattening up
for the regurgitations to come.

The males on this nearly doomed march
lose one-third of their body weight
hitching the eggs along till they hatch,

and then, with nothing to feed the brood,
must vomit what little fluid
they can into those beseeching maws.

Now the macabre dance begins
in the teeth of the polar wind.
It's sheer motion to stay alive:

Starved fathers and unfledged youngsters
in a huddle of down and feathers
shuffle and weave a tight circle

from which some chicks will fall over
and freeze solid, their infant feet
sticking straight up, until the hard night

eases and the ice breaks loose
and waves of mothers rush back,
their blubbery bodies storehouses

of food for the desperate flock.
The males are released for a two-month binge
of Rabelaisian feasting

beyond the ice shelf, barely
enough time to make ready
for the next onslaught of natural

selection, a ten-month struggle
that keeps the species afloat
with purgings and gorgings.

And is there pleasure in it
this bad hand Nature dealt them?
With zoom lenses we look in,

look in and wonder
at what flesh does for them—
we, who are going under.

Thoughts on Saving the Manatee

Weighed down by its dense bones
the manatee swims so slowly
that algae have time to
colonize on its spine.
I know a woman who rode
one down the river gently
scraping with a clamshell
letting drift free a bushel
basket of diatoms and kelp.

At one time you could order
manatee steak in any
restaurant in Florida.
It was said to taste like veal.
My friend reported that hers
bubbled and squealed its pleasure
beneath her making it well
worth risking a five-hundred-
dollar fine for molesting
this cow-size endangered aquatic
mammal whose name derives from
the Carib word for breast.

And from the overlook
at Blue Spring, pendulous
disembodied breasts
are what I see dappling
the play of sunlight on

the lagoon. They swim up here
from the St. Johns River
—mostly cows and their calves—
to disport in the temperate water

and stay to choke on
our discards. They swallow
snarls of fishing line or
the plastic ribbons that tie
beer cans together.
Along with acorns sucked
from the river bottom
they also ingest large numbers
of metal pop tops that razor

their insides. Grazing
on water hyacinths, they're
sideswiped by boat propellers.
Many have bled with bright scars
they come to be known by
and yet, many deaths
are mysterious, if not willful.
Worldwide less than five
thousand manatees remain.

For a small sum you can adopt one
through the Audubons.
Already named Boomer or Jojo
tricked out with a radio collar
it will ascend tranquilized
to be weighed and measured on schedule
but experts agree that no matter

how tenderly tamed by philanthropy
survival is chancy.

Consider my plan.
It's quick and humane:
Let's revert to the Catch of the Day
and serve up the last few as steak marinara.
Let's stop pretending we need them
more than they need us.

Repent

A visual delight,
the killer whale.
Two-tone black and white
from snout to tail.
Worth hunting deep at sea.

And when we've captured two or three
we pen them in a little jail
and teach them tricks
to do for fishy snacks
for paying multitudes who fill

the stands and scream to see
these mammals leap in synchrony,
who cruise a hundred miles a day
when free
beneath the bounding main.

Occasionally from the strain
they turn upon the rubber-suited crew
who labor so to train
them to cavort on cue,
and even maim a few.

Stu-
pidity, said
Immanuel Kant,
is caused by a wicked
heart. Repent.

Homage to Binsey Poplars

O if we but knew what we do
When we delve or hew—

—G. M. Hopkins

The arctic fox of Kiska now is quelled
not spared, not one that preyed upon the goose
the rare Aleutian goose, all, all are felled—

our only white fox (in the winter phase)
swept from the island for the goose's sake
by poison pellets scattered on the ice—

the small endangered goose around whose neck
a narrow ring of white may grow no more
unless the purge of foxes lures it back.

The fox that Russian traders brought ashore
in 1836 to multiply
thence to be harvested year after year

hung leanly on in Kiska till the sly
and fecund Norway rat with nearly nak-
ed tail arrived, shipborne by the Allies.

The rat that fed on garbage stayed to suck
the yolks from eggs, untidy omnivore.
Fox banqueted on goose but kept in check

the Old World rat that bids now to devour
each wished-for clutch on Kiska, to the rue
of federal Fish and Wildlife officers

who, sizing up the prospects of the few
in saving one, eradicated two.

Custodian

Every spring when the ice goes out
black commas come scribbling across the shallows.
Soon they sprout forelegs.
Slowly they absorb their tails
and by mid-June, full-voiced, announce themselves.

Enter our spotted dog.
Every summer, tense with the scent of them,
tail arced like a pointer's but wagging
in anticipation, he stalks his frogs
two hundred yards clockwise around
the perimeter of this mucky pond,
then counterclockwise, an old pensioner
happy in his work.

Once every ten or so pounces
he succeeds, carries his captive north
in his soft mouth, uncorks him on the grass,
and then sits, head cocked, watching the slightly
dazed amphibian hop back to sanctuary.

Over the years the pond's inhabitants
seem to have grown accustomed
to this ritual of capture and release.
They ride untroubled in the wet pocket
of the dog's mouth, disembark in the meadow
like hitchhikers, and strike out again for home.

I have seen others of his species kill
and swallow their catch and then be seized
with violent retchings. I have seen children
corner polliwogs in the sun-flecked hollow
by the green rock and lovingly squeeze
the life out of them in their small fists.
I have seen the great blue heron swoop in
time after wing-slapping time to carry
frogs back to the fledglings in the rookery.

Nothing is to be said here
of need or desire. No moral arises
nor is this, probably, purgatory.
We have this old dog,
custodian of an ancient race of frogs,
doing what he knows how to do
and we too, taking and letting go,
that same story.

Bringing Back the Trumpeter Swan

Sloughs of its down once fell to the prairie, like snow
as it chalked the bright skies of the North Temperate Zone.
Its range was as broad as the roving caribou
and the clack of its wings, as enormous flocks rose up
from trumpeter swan-favored muskegs and swamps,
startled the ear, like the smack of endless home runs.

It didn't take long to endanger the trumpeter swan.
By 1877 the Hudson Bay
Company had sold seventeen thousand skins
mostly for millinery use,
down covers, quill pens, powder puffs
and sundry Victorian *objets.*

In the wild its head and neck are often rust-red
from feeding in ferrous waters. There is
a salmon or flesh-colored stripe, like a fine cord,
at the base of the bill. This is called the grin line.
The voice of the trumpeter swan recalls the klaxon
that used to blare from the perilous taxis of Paris.

The mute swan makes an acceptable foster mother
for the now almost extinct trumpeter swan.
Eggs removed from a captive pair of the latter,
cradled against any possible crush or lurch,
were flown to a sequestered Great Lakes marsh
and inserted into a mute swan's nest, just when

they were thought to be two or three days from date of hatch.
Cygnets first cheep in the shell to establish a bond
with the broody above—essential with this batch.
Don't ask what became of the mute swan's eggs. Don't inquire
about the four hundred snapping turtles speared
from the marsh in advance of the trumpeter swan's

styrofoam-swaddled eggs. Snappers are not
on the endangered list. Never mind—
they're expendable too, the eggs of the mute.
Culling and killing this way, we are bound
to bring back from the brink the trumpeter swan
in the names of Charles Darwin and John James Audubon.

The Accolade of the Animals

All those he never ate
appeared to Bernard Shaw
single file in his funeral
procession as he lay abed
with a cracked infected bone
from falling off his bicycle.
They stretched from Hampton Court
downstream to Piccadilly
against George Bernard's pillow
paying homage to the flesh
of man unfleshed by carnage.

Just shy of a hundred years
of pullets, laying hens
no longer laying, ducks, turkeys,
pigs and piglets, old milk cows,
anemic vealers, grain-fed steer,
the annual Easter lambkin,
the All Hallows' mutton,
ring-necked pheasant, deer,
bags of hare unsnared,
rosy trout and turgid carp
tail-walking like a sketch by Tenniel.

What a cortege it was:
the smell of hay in his nose,
the pungencies of the barn,
the courtyard cobbles slicked
with wet. How we omnivores

suffer by comparison
in the jail of our desires
salivating at the smell of char
who will not live on fruits
and greens and grains alone
so long a life, so sprightly, so cocksure.

Sleeping with Animals

Nightly I choose to keep this covenant
with a wheezing broodmare who, ten days past due,
grunts in her sleep in the vocables
of the vastly pregnant. She lies down
on sawdust of white pine, its turp smell blending
with the rich scent of ammonia and manure.
I in my mummy bag just outside her stall
observe the silence, louder than the catch
in her breathing, observe gradations of
the ancient noneditorial dark; against
the open doorway looking south, observe
the paddock posts become a chain gang, each
one shackled leg and wrist; the pasture wall
a graveyard of bones that ground fog lifts and swirls.

Sleeping with animals,
loving my animals too much,
letting them run like a perfectly detached
statement by Mozart through all the other lines
of my life, a handsome family of serene
horses glistening in their thoughtlessness,
fear ghosts me still for my two skeletons:
one stillborn foal eight years ago.
One, hours old, dead of a broken spine.
Five others swam like divers into air,
dropped on clean straw, were whinnied to, tongued dry,
and staggered, stagey drunkards, to their feet,
nipped and nudged by their mothers to the teat.

Restless, dozy, between occasional coughs
the mare takes note of me and nickers. Heaves
herself up, explores the corners of
her feed tub. Sleeps a little, leg joints locked.
I shine my light across the bar to watch
the immense contours of her flanks rise and fall.
Each double-inhale is threaded to the life
that still holds back in its safe sac.
What we say to each other in the cold black
of April, conveyed in a wordless yet perfect
language of touch and tremor, connects
us most surely to the wet cave we all
once burst from gasping, naked or furred,
into our separate species.

Everywhere on this planet, birth.
Everywhere, curled in the amnion,
an unborn wonder.
Together we wait for this still-clenched burden.

Encounter in August

Black bears are not particularly interested in flesh . . .
they have been seen in the fields eating string beans.

—John McPhee

Inside the tepee that admits
sunlight to the underpart
he stands eating my Kentucky Wonders.
Downs pod after pod, spilling the beans,
the ones I'd saved for shelling out
this winter, thinking *soup*
when he'd gone deep, denned up.

This is not Eden, which ran
unfenced and was not intercropped,
Eden, where frost never overtook a patch.
We stand ten yards apart, two omnivores
not much interested in flesh.
I think he ought to smell me through his greed
or hear my heart outbeat his steady chomp

but nothing interrupts his lunch.
At last he goes the way the skunk
does, supreme egoist, ambling
into the woodlot on all fours
leaving my trellis flat and beanless
and yet I find the trade-off fair:
beans and more beans for this hour of bear.

Catchment

When the she-leopard stalks and pounces on
an infant antelope, which one
am I rooting for? The newborn

I saw slip, moments ago, free
from the birth canal, struggle to its feet,
stagger against its mother's teat

and begin to nurse, both nervously
twitching tail stubs in the heat
and flies of the equator

or the big cat, in whose camouflaged lair
three helpless youngsters wait
so starved for meat that she dares

venture out to hunt by daylight?
I watch this living-color film unfold
with a friend, whose English bull

mastiff pup—as if
New Hampshire were the veldt, as if
its life depended on the chase—

leapt up last month to snatch
a newborn doe kid from her arms
and snapped its neck with one good shake.

Later, watching the after-afterglow
flush the whole sky pink, then darken,
we can almost discuss it, good and harm.

Nature a catchment of sorrows.
We hug each other. No lesson drawn.

On Reading an Old Baedeker in Schloss Leopoldskron

Salzburg, Austria

Soft as beetpulp, the cover
of this ancient Baedeker.
The gold print has scabbed off the leather
but thirty-three tissue paper maps extend
from Vienna to Bosnia. One
of my grandfathers is in here somewhere
living in three rooms over his tailor
shop on the Judengasse in Salzburg or
Prague, stitching up frock coats on Jew
Alley in Pilsen, or in the mews
of Vienna's Old Quarter,
my mother's loyal obsequious *Opa*
tugging his forelock whenever
the name of Franz Joseph is spoken.

In this edition you can still travel
by diligence down from Bad Ischl
to Hallstatt, where grottoes full of bones
of early Celt miners have been uncovered.
Whole families journey to see them
cycling single file, observing the caution
to keep to the left "because in
whatever part of the Empire you meet them,
troops on the march, sized by height
and moving smartly, always keep right."

Not for you, *Opa*, this tourist attraction,
punts lapping the stone-green lake in

the hanging valley of Hallstatt,
languorous voices hovering
adrift in dappled sunlight
and the Lionel-toy train tunneling
out of its papier-mâché mountain
to pause at the cardboard station
where day trippers, disembarking,
may visit the fake antique ruin,
a mossed-over stucco *folly.*
Time to shoulder your knapsack
and strike out for Ellis Island.
Kiss your nine sisters and never look back.

Never look back, Grandfather.
Don't catch my eye on this marble
staircase as wide as the 'gasse
you lived in. Don't look at the chandeliers
that shone on the Nazi Gauleiter
who moved in and made this headquarters.
Here in the cavernous Great Hall
I look for some thin line of comfort
that binds us, some weight-bearing bridge

and finally walk out in rain
to fling stale rolls to the swans
in their ninetieth generation.

The Festung, Salzburg

I shall have to pee out the window, says the translation
in the 1902 pocket phrasebook Alastair's
grandfather gave him. Also, *Call the hostler!*
and *Here are my boots,* meaning polish them
but nothing that helps decipher life in this fortress
four hundred years ago, all cobble and cannon,
all ice storms and armor and horses. How, for example,
did they haul water for livestock and people?
Out of what reservoir make time for
carving twelve marble apostles and a Christ
that are tucked in a chapel chipped from the rock
of the scarp that commands the Salzach?
No idiom to tell us how secure
this Festung was before war took the air.

Down in the candybox town we dawdle
at Tomaselli's over cups of hot chocolate.
I pretend I have come back here for the sake
of my forebears, come back out of exile
to reinvent how it was for them,
seeking among the faces that pass
those as old as I, those few with missing
limbs, or sightless, who endured the Anschluss,
seeking among the dirndls and lederhosen
the unknowable middle-aged ones who risked the ovens
and came through stained with a deep understanding.
Bitte, bitte schön. Ropes of rain
fall on a sea of purposeful umbrellas
in calm green homogeneous Austria.

Night Launch

Canaveral Seashore National Park

Full moon. Everyone in silhouette
graying just this side of color as we wait:
babies in Snuglis, toddlers from whose clutches
ancient blankets depend, adults encumbered
with necklaces of cameras, binoculars.
A city of people gathered on the beach.
Expectant boats jockeying offshore.

When we were kids we used to race
reciting *the seething sea ceaseth;*
thus the sea sufficeth us
and then collapse with laughter, never
having seen the rise-and-fall of ocean,
the lip of foam like seven-minute icing,
moon-pricked dots of plankton skittering.

The horizon opens, floods with daybreak,
a rosy sunrise as out of sync
as those you fly into crossing the Atlantic,
midnight behind you, the bald sky blank,
and up comes the shuttle, one costly Roman candle,
orange, silent, trailing as its rockets fall
away, a complicated snake of vapor.

Along the beach a feeble cheer.
Muffled thumps of blastoff, long after,
roll like funeral drums, precise and grave.
We are the last to leave.
Driving back along the asphalt, signed

every hundred yards Evacuation Route
past honeycombs of concrete condominiums
I remember how we wrapped and carried
our children out to a suburban backyard
to see Sputnik cross the North Temperate Zone
at two in the morning, and how we shivered
watching that unwinking little light
move east without apparent cause.
On this warm seacoast tonight
in the false dawn my neckhairs rose.
Danger flew up to uncertain small applause.

Photograph, Maryland Agricultural College Livestock Show, 1924

Blond, wholesome, serene,
their white shirtsleeves rolled,
these boys in white ducks
keep sleek black hogs at their feet,
hogs cleaner than licorice sticks in the sun.
Five haltered calves are also held
in tandem while their names
and pedigrees are said aloud.

Mostly I think about
the unseen mud and manure, flies
and screwworms that connect these boys
and their wildest hopes
poised radiant between two wars
while just out of reach of the lens
in their stained bib overalls
stand the farm laborers

greasy with sweat
and undoubtedly black.

Photograph, U.S. Army Flying School, College Park, Maryland, 1909

Wilbur Wright is racing the locomotive
on the Baltimore and Ohio commuter line.
The great iron horse hisses and hums on its rails
but the frail dragonfly overhead appears to be winning.
Soon we will have dog fights and the Red Baron.
The firebombing of Dresden is still to come.
And the first two A-bombs, all that there are.

The afterburners of jets lie far in the future
and the seeds of our last descendants, who knows,
are they not yet stored in their pouches?

On Being Asked to Write a Poem in Memory of Anne Sexton

The elk discards his antlers every spring.
They rebud, they grow, they are growing

an inch a day to form a rococo rack
with a five-foot spread even as we speak:

cartilage at first, covered with velvet;
bendable, tender gristle, yet

destined to ossify, the velvet sloughed off,
hanging in tatters from alders and scrub growth.

No matter how hardened it seems there was pain.
Blood on the snow from rubbing, rubbing, rubbing.

What a heavy candelabrum to be borne
forth, each year more elaborately turned:

the special issues, the prizes in her name.
Above the mantel the late elk's antlers gleam.

In the Park

You have forty-nine days between
death and rebirth if you're a Buddhist.
Even the smallest soul could swim
the English Channel in that time
or climb, like a ten-month-old child,
every step of the Washington Monument
to travel across, up, down, over or through
—you won't know till you get there which to do.

He laid on me for a few seconds
said Roscoe Black, who lived to tell
about his skirmish with a grizzly bear
in Glacier Park. *He laid on me*
not doing anything. I could feel
his heart beating against my heart.
Never mind *lie* and *lay*, the whole world
confuses them. For Roscoe Black you might say
all forty-nine days flew by.

I was raised on the Old Testament.
In it God talks to Moses, Noah,
Samuel, and they answer.
People confer with angels. Certain
animals converse with humans.
It's a simple world, full of crossovers.
Heaven's an airy Somewhere, and God
has a nasty temper when provoked,
but if there's a Hell, little is made of it.
No longtailed Devil, no eternal fire,

and no choosing what to come back as.
When the grizzly bear appears, he lies/lays down
on atheist and zealot. In the pitch-dark
each of us waits for him in Glacier Park.

Marianne, My Mother, and Me

I close the book I am reading in which
there's a picnic in the country before the Great War.
William Carlos Williams has motored over
from Rutherford and lots of the Greenwich
Village crowd come up with cheese and bread
and Marianne Moore arrives with her bright red hair
in braids wound twice around her head,

as long as that. She's the same age as my mother,
who deftly plays four hands at the piano
in the Conservatory and flirts so
outrageously she has to elope with my father.
At this picnic, Alfred Kreymborg—it's his place—
hands around the stuffed eggs and everyone
sits on the ground in attitudes of such grace
that tears come into my eyes for what is gone,

for the intensity of it, I think I mean,
the way the poets turn up in each other's
richly detailed literary memoirs
making the dangerous era we live in seem
pallid, empty at least of artistic passion.
That same year my father buys a Stanley Steamer.
He and my mother wheel past, the toast of the town
in their matching linen dusters and gay demeanor,

but this perfect picture is flawed with spider cracks.
His only brother is soon to be gassed at the Marne.
My housebound mother, crazed with her first-born,

opens the lid of the Steinway with an axe.
Nevertheless, the next babe and the next and next
come forth in jig time, though Pa, ascending
among the nouveaux riches on Wall Street specs,
is seldom home. Released from baby-tending

by a starchy Nanny, Momma finds renown
as a demon shopper. Chopin is packed away.
A wet bar flows in the space of the vanquished Steinway
and obsequious salesladies all over town
call up to describe designer frocks on sale.
Meanwhile, Marianne's father, in despair
over his failure to provide the wherewithal
for his family, blinks twice and disappears.

Our heroine, undaunted, graduates
from Bryn Mawr and teaches stenography
in an American Indian school upstate,
becomes a librarian, an editor, and inch
by inch the closet poet emerges. "We
must be as clear as our natural reticence
will allow," she announces. Rapturously

I try this statement on like a negligee
that's neither diaphanous nor yet opaque.
Crisp lyrics from her quirky intellect
flare across Modern Poetry Survey
where she's sandwiched between Pound and Ransom.
But not once in my four years as a Cliffie,
humble in Harvard Yard, do I find that phantom
I long for, a woman professor, trailed by her covey.

Pearl Harbor bursts apart. Cambridge fills
with uniforms. How to accommodate
the life of the mind with the inmost patriot?
Six days a week at dawn in Sever Hall
toward that end, I take intensive Russian
with crewcut PFC's quickmarched from barracks.
My mother attends air raid warden sessions.
Marianne writes "In Distrust of Merits":

Strengthened to live, strengthened to die, for medals . . .
My brothers ship out, each to a different theater.
Sunlight glints on the B School's 90-day wonders,
those all-boy ensigns. I try for the WACs but am stalled.
Hiroshima melts down. Sweet peace, reprieve.
Marianne embarks on La Fontaine.
I graduate, get married; *too young*, Mother weeps,
and yet we're liver-spotted with dead friends.

Soon after, my mother's a volunteer. She reads
to the blind, pricks Beethoven in braille, makes
weekly side trips to the Philharmonic
and suddenly it's the fifties. I've become
a freshman English instructor, a freshman poet
as well. Marianne is reading her poems
at Wellesley. Surely the ones I know by heart

will trickle through the leaky microphone.
My fingers riffle pages of the texts
but the black tricorn bending low deflects
that flat small voice from reaching anyone.
I tell myself, it's like Faulkner's "The Bear":

You must relinquish everything to enter
into its presence. Except that having come there
I'm eye to eye with what? An eccentric spinster

whom I can't emulate, however much
I admire her words that "cluster like chromosomes."
Strong emotion has no place in her poems
but slithers into every line I touch.
We never meet. I am content to take
to heart her praise of idiosyncrasy,
exactitude, intensity, technique.
Her "be accurate and modest" speaks to me.

When Robert Lowell puffs her as "the best
woman poet in English," I thrill to hear
Langston Hughes's riposte: "I consider her
[it's 1953] the most famous
Negro woman poet in America."
A vintage year—my third child is born.
From her grandmother bracelet, nine criteria
of my mother's worth dangle, each name a charm.

Here's Marianne posing for *Life* magazine
at the zoo. Here, rooting for the Brooklyn Dodgers.
Here, *The New Yorker* prints an exchange of letters
between the poet and the corporate machine
as Ford invites Miss Moore to find a name
for its disastrous Edsel. None of hers
would do, though fanciful and fleet of limb.
The sixties roll round. My first book appears.

This is the decade in which assassination
catches on, like a vile pop tune. We mourn

a president who was briefly everyone's darling.
We mourn his brother. Sexton and I in the rain
sway with thousands on Boston Common
to hear Martin Luther King. And then we lose him
and lose Evers and Schwerner, Cheney, and Goodman
and all of us lose heart in Vietnam.

Little from Marianne of praise or caveat
in these years. Reviewing a new anthology
she opens herself to report that Allen G.
"can foul the nest in a way to marvel at,"
but nothing she says impinges on events.
"Greed seems to me the vice of the century,"
she writes in *Seventeen.* On a Central Park bench
she poses with Mickey Spillane for an airline venture,

not for the fee from Braniff, but because it feels
impolite to her to refuse. My mother, I'm sure
would agree. I wonder, at that early *déjeuner sur
l'herbe,* can Marianne turn down the wassail?
Over the years each tries on rich disguises.
The poet becomes her beasts in armor and shell,
a woman adept at the wittiest camouflages
but under them always lurks the shy red-haired girl

while my mother pretends not to find old age bewildering.
Widowed, she takes up art. She goes on cruises.
Snapshots of the several great-grandchildren
accompany her. Though she hears less and less
she keeps her Friday seat at Symphony
and keeps the program notes, along with clips
of my reviews. Thus pass the seventies.
The end's in sight. First Marianne slips

away, original and last of her line.
Soon after, my mother, the dowager queen
leaving behind descendants like a string
of worry beads. I claim them both as mine
whose lives began in a gentler time and place
of horse-drawn manners, parlor decorum
—though no less stained with deception and regret—
before man split the atom, thrust the jet,
procured the laser, shot himself through space,
both shapers of my alphabet.

A Calling

Over my desk Georgia O'Keeffe says
I have no theories to offer and then
takes refuge in the disembodied
third person singular: *One works*
I suppose because it is the most
interesting thing one knows to do.
O Georgia! Sashaying between
first base and shortstop as it were
drawing up a list of all the things
one imagines one has to do . . .
You get the garden planted. You
take the dog to the vet. You
certainly have to do the shopping.

Syntax, like sex, is intimate.
One doesn't lightly leap from person
to person. *The painting,* you said,
is like a thread that runs
through all the reasons for all the other
things that make one's life.
O awkward invisible third person,
come out, stand up, be heard!
Poetry is like farming. It's
a calling, it needs constancy,
the deep woods drumming of the grouse,
and long life, like Georgia's, who
is talking to one, talking to me,
talking to you.

Turning the Garden in Middle Age

They have lain a long time, these two:
parsnip with his beard on his foot,
puddingstone with fool's gold in her ear
until, under the thrust of my fork,
earthlock lets go. Mineral
and marrow are flung loose in May
still clinging together as if
they had intended this embrace.

I think then of skulls picked clean
underground, and the long bones
of animals overturned in the woods
and the gorgeous insurgency
of these smart green weeds
erect now in every furrow
that lure me once more
to set seeds in the loam.

Reviewing the Summer and Winter Calendar of the Next Life

If death comes in July, they'll put me down
for barn swallow, consigned to an 18-hour
day of swoopings and regurgitations.
No sooner the first set of fledglings lined up
five perfect clones on the telephone wire
than another quartet of eggs erupts in the slap-
dab nest. *Is there no rest in this life?*
the parents beseech each time I forget
not to open the door under their house
attached to the porch stringers. Even the dog
slinks past when they dive, scolding, clearing the stage
for their juveniles finally flapping aloft.

If January, I'll get to pick and choose
among the evening grosbeaks bombing the feeder
in a savage display of yellow scapulars
or return as a wild-turkey, one of the brace
who come at a waddle at 10 a.m.
punctual comics, across the manure pile
for their illicit fix of feedbin corn
or join the juncos, whose job description involves
sweeping up after everybody else,
even venturing in to dust the stalls
of the barn for stray or recycled specks of grain.

I only ask not ever to come back as
weasel, present but seldom seen in summer
darting from rock to hummock in his tacky fur.
Reptilian, equally slim of head and hip,

he can be caught sight of at ten below
stained dingy white in his unbleached muslin cape.
Rat-toothed egg-sucker, making do
like any desperate one of us, he slips
through the least crack into the food chain
chipping and chewing his way past links of rust
to claim our kingdom for his own.

Grappling in the Central Blue

Benevolent blue air
of October
I take you into custody
as I do the memories
of 1940 and before—
the unemployed uncles
hangdog in the yard
playing touch football
shooting squirrels
Elmer Davis and the bad news
crackling through Bakelite—
when we did not know
we were waiting for war.

I declare you
Month I Will Not Let Go Of
October
I take you into my arms
even as festoons
of mushrooms, adorned beneath
with accordion-pleated gills
attack the punky elms
and fasten on their decay.
Year after year
in one part of the woodland
they erupt from the bark
in elaborate layers.

Dropkicked the football
goes tacking
across the yard from
Oscar to Dan to Joe
the air full of their breathing
their roughneck calls
the ballet
of their ankles and elbows
those bad boys my father
despairs of ever unhousing
and their Cuba Libras
(his rum) safely behind
the clothesline goalposts.

One is to die by torpedo.
One in a swamp on maneuvers.
Only the oldest, at a great age
a child again, outlasts my father
to drift off alone in bed.
What awaits us
is hardly to be thought of.
Let us eat of the inland oyster.
Let its fragrance intoxicate us
into almost believing
that staying on is possible
again this year in
benevolent blue October.

The Bangkok Gong

Home for a visit, you brought me
a circle of hammered brass
reworked from an engine part
into this curio
to be struck with a wad of cotton
pasted onto a stick.
Third World ingenuity
you said, reminds you
of Yankee thrift.

The tone of this gong
is gentle, haunting, but
hard struck three times
can call out as far
as the back fields
to say Supper
or, drummed darkly,
Blood everywhere!
Come quick.

When barely touched it imitates
the deep nicker the mare makes
swiveling her neck
watching the foal swim
out of her body.
She speaks to it even as
she pushes the hindlegs clear.
Come to me is her message
as they curl to reach each other.

Now that you are
back on the border
numbering the lucky ones
whose visas let them
leave everything behind
except nightmares, I hang
the gong on my doorpost.
Some days I
barely touch it.

We Stood There Singing

On a gray day in March in his first year
we drove up out of orderly Geneva
mother and daughter and the daughter's child
up the hairpin turns of the Chasseral
in search of the horses of the Franches-Montagnes
with feathered fetlocks and manes blown wild
each splashed-white face the same, the same kind eye
said to persist unchanged since Charlemagne.

The baby slept tipped sideways in his chair
slept through sudden snow squalls that blanked
the alpine road like a stage scrim
and woke up cranky in Les Breûleux where
at the village's one store we stopped to take
our bearings. When he howled, the aproned woman
invited us back, past vats of sauerkraut
and wheels of cheese into their bedroom.

I remember that plain space of rough white plaster
oaken crucifix, oak beams overhead
runner of tatted lace on the chest of drawers.
I remember the lambskin she unrolled on the bed
motioning you to lay him down, and after
he was done up sweet with powder, she opened her arms
and bounced him chortling around the room
singing him bits of *le bon roi Dagobert.*

We stood there singing.
I remember
that moment of civility among women.

Distance

What does it mean, I ask myself, while I am mowing
with the Tuff-Cut, slicing through a sprawl
of buttercups, graying pussytoes, and the unfurled
pale green tongues of milkweed in the pasture, how
do I, who buried both my parents long ago,
attach my name and number to another birthday?

Whoever mows with a big machine like this,
with two forward speeds and a wheel clutch, nippled hand
grips,
a lever to engage the cutting blade, is androgynous
as is old age, especially for us marathoners.

We are growing into one sex, a little leathery
but loving, appreciating the air of midday
embroidered with leaping insects, the glint glancing from
the flanks of grazing horses, the long puppyhood of the
young.

Around me old friends (and enemies) are beleaguered
with cancer or clogged arteries. I ought to be
melancholy inching upward through my sixties
surrounded by the ragged edges of so many acres,
parlaying the future with this aerobic mowing,
but I take courage from a big wind staving off the deerflies,

ruffling and parting the grasses like a cougar if there
were still cougars. I am thankful for what's left that's wild:
the coydogs who howl in unison when a distant fire siren

or the hoot owl starts them up, the moose that muddled
through the winter in the swampland behind us, the bears
that drop their spoor studded with cherry pits in our swales.

If I could free a hand behind this Tuff-Cut
I'd tug my forelock at the sow and her two cubs I met
at high noon last week on the trail to Bible Hill.
Androgyny. Another birthday. And all the while
the muted roar of satisfactory machinery.
May we flourish and keep our working distance.

A Game of Monopoly in Chavannes

Each time I look up from the board to the rusty vineyards
I can see, through mist like grains of finest pollen
large dogs being walked, straining against their collars.

Higher up in the Jura, a light snow, *un peu timide*
they say here, sifts down on rounded humps of hills.
The chic white lacquered table we sit around,

three generations, smells of newness still.
It came in parts, like a child's intricate toy.
Assembling it was an hour's play . . . In my mind

I've landed on Boardwalk again and cannot pay,
the Bank is cheating me blind, it's the late thirties.
Too young to do sums, I am almost always in tears.

My brothers, two cousins and I, unaware
we are sent here each summer out of filial duty
squabble over St. James Place and the Short Line

in our grandmother's fusty Atlantic Avenue flat.
From Oma's front room overlooking the Boardwalk
we can hear the surf break and sigh sucking back

but we're unaware of the irony of place:
cheap haven for the Depression's pensioners.
To us Atlantic City is paradise

except when it rains like this, except when we hear
Oma's foreign words that speak pain and terror.
We buck up to decide whose turn to roll the dice

on the massive bleached oak table scrubbed with lemon
its six carved legs ending in jungly claws . . .
My grandson's in Jail. He has failed three times

to throw releasing doubles. He has failed
to pass Go, lost two hundred dollars, and then
having paid his fine, lands on Luxury Tax.

His lower lip trembles, this luxury of a child
who burst naked into our lives, like luck.
Our sole inheritor, he has taken us over

with his oceanic wants, his several passports.
I will deed him the Reading Railroad, the Water Works,
the Electric Company, my hotel on Park Place.

All that I have is his, under separate cover
and we are the mortgaged nub of all that he has.
Soon enough he will learn, buying long, selling short

his ultimate task is to stay to usher us out.

Index

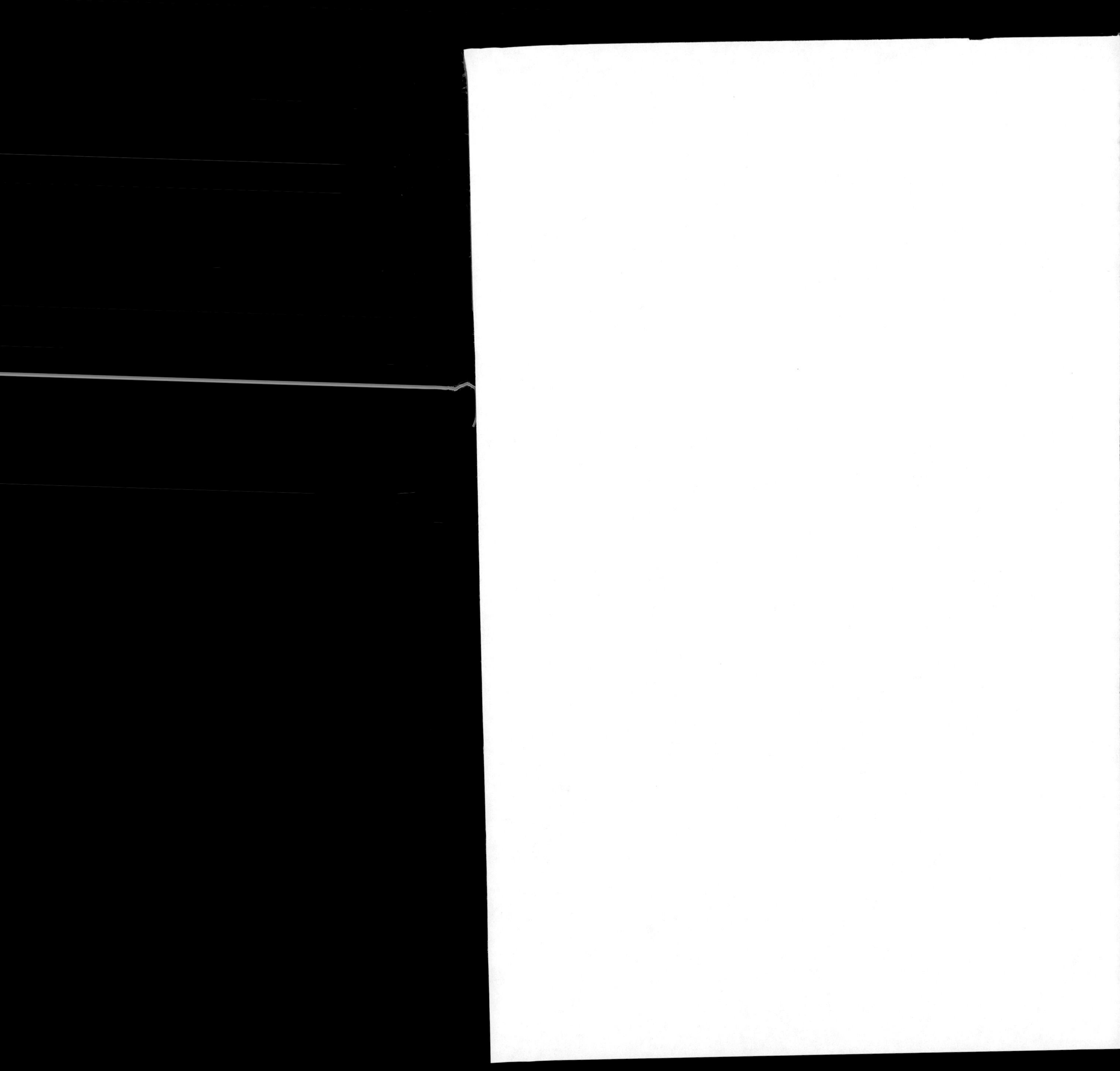